GUERRILLA NATION

GUERRILLA NATION

My Wars
In and Out
of Vietnam

MICHAEL MACLEAR

DUNDURN
TORONTO

Editor: Allister Thompson
Design: Jesse Hooper
Printer: Webcom

Library and Archives Canada Cataloguing in Publication

Maclear, Michael, author
     Guerrilla nation : my wars in and out of Vietnam / by Michael Maclear.

Includes index.
Issued in print and electronic formats.
ISBN 978-1-4597-0940-9 (bound).--ISBN 978-1-4597-0941-6 (pdf).--ISBN 978-1-4597-0942-3 (epub)

     1. Maclear, Michael. 2. Vietnam War, 1961-1975. 3. War correspondents--Canada--Biography. 4. Journalists--Canada--Biography.I. Title.

PN4913.M365A3 2013   070.92   C2013-900905-1
                                                                C2013-900906-X

1   2   3   4   5   17   16   15   14   13

We acknowledge the support of the **Canada Council for the Arts** and the **Ontario Arts Council** for our publishing program. We also acknowledge the financial support of the **Government of Canada** through the **Canada Book Fund** and **Livres Canada Books,** and the **Government of Ontario** through the **Ontario Book Publishing Tax Credit** and the **Ontario Media Development Corporation.**

Care has been taken to trace the ownership of copyright material used in this book. The author and the publisher welcome any information enabling them to rectify any references or credits in subsequent editions.

J. Kirk Howard, President

Visit us at
Dundurn.com | @dundurnpress | Facebook.com/dundurnpress | Pinterest.com/dundurnpress

Dundurn	Gazelle Book Services Limited	Dundurn
3 Church Street, Suite 500	White Cross Mills	2250 Military Road
Toronto, Ontario, Canada	High Town, Lancaster, England	Tonawanda, NY
M5E 1M2	L41 4XS	U.S.A. 14150

Dedicated to the Beaconsfield Four

CONTENTS

AUTHOR'S NOTE

FOR THE WAR CORRESPONDENT in television's pre-satellite years, getting the story was only half the battle — getting it out often the hardest part. But as the only Western journalist filming in North Vietnam during the war's climactic years, I'd find a troubling third dimension: getting the story believed!

Back then, I thought the way I got into Hanoi was rough enough, but the really rough stuff came from the Nervous Nellie that was the Canadian Broadcasting Corporation in those years. Here, I must stress that the mindset of early CBC management, as experienced by the author and told here for the first time, is in *no* way a profile of, or reflection on the matured, highly professional CBC of today, nor has any person at CBC participated in this narrative in any manner at any time. This telling of events almost five decades ago amounts to a pretty decent interval for a decidedly un-pretty story, but lessons are always timely! Be it the wars of nations or corporations, *Guerrilla Nation* is an alert for today, whether for politicians or historians, or simply for every television news viewer, which is just about all of us!

For the foreign correspondent, risking the wrath of home base goes with the territory — at least when reporting unpopular facts. My war in and out of Vietnam portrays a "Cult of Management," motivated, as I saw it, more by self-preservation than by its duty to the public. And since that's a failing that could occur anywhere, in any sector at any time, consider this narrative just an example, with the CBC hereafter broadly, distantly named The Network.

— Michael Maclear, September 2013

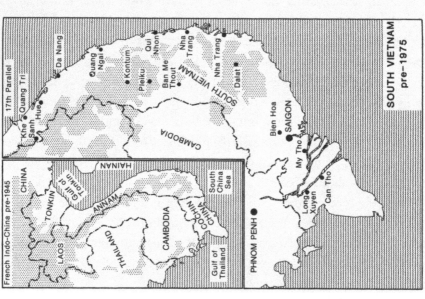

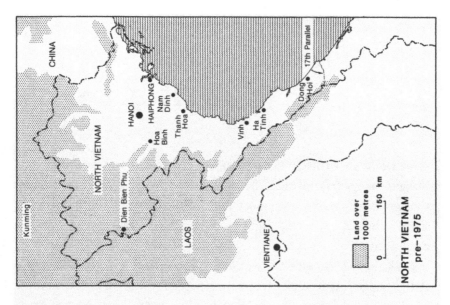

NORTH VIETNAM
pre–1975

Land over
1000 metres

0   150 km

SOUTH VIETNAM
pre–1975

French Indo-China pre-1945

CHAPTER ONE
Into the Unknown

AS ALWAYS, IN RETURNING to Vietnam there's so much of the unexpected. In Hanoi, where shoals of cyclists once gracefully glided, armadas of Hondas now ceaselessly roar, their young riders totally consumer-driven with minimal interest in their nation's guerrilla past — a hopeful sign that today's bloody insurgencies may yet conclude the same way. Today, in the new 'Nam of the second decade of the twenty-first century, all the world's great brand names line streets once flattened by B-52s. After all, it did not need Western bombs to instil Western ways!

Unlike its old adversary, Vietnam has moved on. War is the distant past, a subject for students, not soldiers. Indeed, I am back in Hanoi as one such student, here to fill in the gaps of my wartime knowledge of the guerrilla nation. Now, some forty years since I was first in the North, the senior military commanders of the Ho Chi Minh Trail had agreed to candid interviews. I can but hope that this time their revelations will be believed!

In the war years, my wartime reports of an "enemy" more nationalist than Marxist had increasingly incensed the White House, so that finally my own network openly displayed its uncertainty about my Vietnam reportage and then soon after, over a dispute on Middle East coverage, summarily dismissed me as their London-based correspondent without a hearing, and this after fifteen years as a foreign correspondent. Time had not erased the memories, nor should it, for the Network by its actions not least betrayed its public.

Yet back in Vietnam, everything else forgotten, I was once again in a bouncing jeep heading toward the legendary Ho Chi Minh Trail.

A large part of the legend, though little known outside Vietnam, is General Dong Sy Nguyen, overall commander of the "Trail," the Western name for the Truong Son ("Long Mountains") which stretch like a spine the length of the former Indo-China. Today, it is again one of the least inhabited, most perilous regions on Earth, but the general had lived there under constant aerial attack, in ever shifting headquarters deep in the dense forests, for eleven years (1962–73). I had seen a film of him at the time when viewing Hanoi's military archives: a tall, Zorro-like figure, without the mask but always wearing a dark, flowing cape.

Meeting me at his new barracks near the Trail, he wore simple light khaki without medals and with a manner just as modest. Yet this was the man who had a personal knowledge of guerrilla tactics unequalled in modern history. Just meeting him evoked a sense of entering the unknown, and perhaps because he had watched the thirteen-hour history series *Vietnam: The Ten Thousand Day War*, which I had conceived and written, seeing how American military leaders had spoken so readily and fully, he too felt the same need to ease the burden of memory. I started by asking when and how the war on the Trail began. He explained that after the defeat of the colonial French army at Dien Bien Phu in May 1954, the Great Powers meeting in Geneva had partitioned Vietnam but pledged national elections within two years (a peace settlement which the United States did not sign). Ho Chi Minh, certain to have won the election, waited three more years, then in great secrecy and to circumvent partition, ordered a small team of cadres and geologists to explore a Truong Son route to the southern delta as the only means of arming the fledgling National Liberation Front, or Viet Cong. That first journey took them six months.

Ho chose the code name 559 for the starting date of the mission: May 1959, a date that resonated with me since it was the exact time I first visited South Vietnam, casually travelling through the countryside but finding no danger, only rumours of war. In fact, for some years only a few cadres infiltrated south. It was 1962, said the general, when the first troops were sent, on foot all the way, and it took them four months, braving killer monsoons, malaria, and snakes whose bite could kill in seconds. By spring '63, enough dirt roads had been fashioned for a few primitive trucks, but "the quantity of guns and ammunition sent was limited and we must admit that we suffered large casualties. There were days, even weeks when we got stuck, not able to move at all; days when we lost hundreds of our soldiers to aerial attacks."

Again, I remembered at this time being back in Saigon as anti-war Buddhist monks began gruesome self-immolation, remembered U.S. Ambassador Henry Cabot Lodge gazing horrified at a charred body, saying to the gathered press "This must end." Soon after, Saigon's President was assassinated by his own generals at a time when President John F. Kennedy, also assassinated weeks later, was believed ready to write off Vietnam.

From what General Dong Sy Nguyen told me, the North as well as the South were hurting so badly in mid-1963 that peace of a kind seemed possible, but the next year President Lyndon Johnson ordered Rolling Thunder, all-out bombing of the "Trail" and the bordering provinces. By then, I'd become the Network's London correspondent, but through a highly placed contact I kept applying to Hanoi for a press visa, never really expecting to get one, since no journalist had in recent years.

In the decade that followed, the "Trail" grew from a mere footpath to a grid of paved roads and support hideouts extending over 13,500 kilometres, or ten times the Truong Son's geographical length. It was evolving far beyond U.S. intelligence estimates and in a form beyond imagination. Simply put, General Nguyen's solution for protracted war was to bring the city to the jungle. With meticulous organization, he set up ten key departments under separate commands: for vehicle transport, communications, mapmaking, sappers, artillery, infantry, signal corps, medical corps, and, perhaps the most vital of all, bunker design. Later, field clinics and rest facilities — all coded by numbers — were added every few miles, with the general keeping the Ho Chi Minh code 559 for his main headquarters located, he told me, at Sepon (Tchepone) on the Lao side of the Truong Son. Over time, his guerrilla force became so sophisticated it had pipelines for water and for gasoline stretching hundreds of miles wherever the forests gave cover. Like the GIs in the South, the guerrillas had their own currency, their own news weeklies, their own mail system and parcel delivery.

All this information was totally new to anything I learned or observed during my wartime coverage of North Vietnam, but the wry thought occurred that all this would anyhow have been dismissed by the Pentagon — like my other reports — as "pinko crap" with my own Network echoing, "Were you duped?"

Impressed by the general's tell-all information, I asked him what the Pentagon back then had been pondering for years after. "How many troops went down the Trail?"

He answered without hesitation: "*Hai trieu.*"

I asked the interpreter, "Did he say two million?"

And then, on camera, the general repeated more fully, "The number of troops from the North that went through to the South during those years was about two million."

Assuming this number is accurate, it means that in Vietnam the U.S was never prepared for, or aware of, the extent of guerrilla infiltration. General Nguyen was telling me that over the decade 1963–73 an average two hundred thousand troops went down the Trail each year, with the number obviously much higher in the later years. U.S. intelligence estimates ranged from sixty to eighty thousand a year troop infiltration, yet at the same time some military experts were calculating a need for ten-to-one troop superiority to contain or counter the estimated guerrilla numbers. So, on that basis, and if accepting the infiltration rate of two hundred thousand a year, the U.S., even with its air dominance, would have needed two million troops rather than its peak force of 570,000 to defend the South.

Yet the general's numbers had to have meant staggering losses. Given these, how much longer could morale have been sustained? He answered, saying "Our soldiers realized there were two possibilities for them — either not being able to go back [home], or winning the war and going back." However difficult to comprehend, it is this readiness to die for a cause — albeit causes totally different — that links the Vietnam of yesterday to the wars of today.

Superior firepower and ever newer military technology has yet to prove an answer to determined guerrilla war, though I was to learn that in Vietnam it came dramatically close — with the North at one time fearing that "all was lost"!

Everything depended on supply trucks dodging aerial attacks for a thousand miles or more, *every day*, year after year, so I next went to meet the man who, through largely primitive means, had to outwit history's mightiest superpower.

Like the general, Colonel Phan Huu Dai readily revealed some of the greatest secrets of the war. He had commanded three vehicle transport divisions, the trucks which continuously ran the greatest gauntlet ever known (well, except maybe that of crossing the streets in post-war Hanoi!). Colonel Dai had invited me to his home, but in making my way there the war and its dangers paled against the peril of onrushing Hondas! Now it seemed the entire post-war generation was motorized, each with shoulder-slung laptops assuring them of their daily fix of celebrity gossip from the land their fathers had fought so long to repel.

But in the colonel's living room the reality and perplexity of the one-time guerrilla nation returned. He told me he had lived on the Trail for ten years, his command one of ten self-sustaining armies of the forest, but perhaps the highest-risk of them all. He had started out with just a dozen or so outdated trucks, but by the late sixties had a reserve of three thousand trucks constantly replenished by China and the Soviet Union. As a routine, a hundred trucks ran the U.S. aerial gauntlet each day.

On average, it needed only twenty or so trucks, bearing troops and arms, to get through to the southern delta to sustain the guerrilla war. Over a decade, he said his division lost some fifteen thousand trucks and twenty thousand drivers — which didn't include undisclosed casualties of the many truckloads of troops.

Every so often, in describing the battles of the Trail, the colonel would slip a DVD into a laptop placed on a low table beneath a large portrait of Ho Chi Minh. These scenes (of which he gave me copies) had been filmed for High Command assessment and were more graphic than anything I'd seen before. Only now, four decades later, could I sense the price paid, with never an end in sight, by the armies of the North.

At key junctions on the Trail, entire areas of forest had become a chemically poisoned wasteland of ashen grey. Here, like so many dead sentinels, giant trees stripped of all foliage rose naked to the sky, while with seeming madness howling fighter jets dived at exposed troop-laden trucks speeding for survival along a cratered dirt road. Every so often, a truck would explode and the ceaseless AA barrage would also make a kill. So it went on the Trail for some four thousand days.

"Have you ever been back?" I asked Colonel Dai.

"Impossible — it's now as it was originally, almost impenetrable. Look," and he inserted a much different disk. Now we gazed at recent aerial film of the Truong Son, and everywhere we saw an immensity of green. Somehow, miraculously, nature had healed itself. The sight of this clearly moved the colonel. No matter if today's youth viewed it all dispassionately. He and his generation, against all odds, had prevailed on the Trail — and the restored Truong Son was their eternal testimonial.

"Was there ever any doubt?" I asked. And when he replied, I felt once again the journalistic thrill of the unknown.

He hesitated for a while, then said, "Early 1971, we were in a state of utter confusion, all seemed lost," and though I rapidly took notes, personal memories took over: early 1971, the time of my last days with the Network after so much mutual distrust that began with the strangest of journeys at the most divisive of times, when 'Nam confounded us all.

In the hundred-degree late summer heat at Vientiane, the weight of my two huge suitcases was unbearable. But carry them I must!

Even for this decidedly odd corner of the world, it was one of the stranger sights: a tall, lone figure staggering across the tarmac of Wattay Airport toward the ancient Boeing 307, still a hundred yards ahead. Half my mind was on making it to the Boeing, half on how if need be I'd explain this latest escapade to Management. Behind me, curious spectators emerged from the terminal building: Soviet types wearing standard black suits so cheap they rumpled right off the rack, and U.S. Embassy Third Secretaries, young and devout theorists on winning wars they never actually experienced.

And standing apart, flaunting full holsters, were the pilots of the CIA-owned Air America, the Dakota gunships which I could see openly parked beyond my Boeing. I glanced back, noting the terminal's apocryphal slogan, "Land of a Million Elephants." Land of a Million Spooks described Laos better. Every major power had its quota of spies here, all of them forever snooping on each other, scouting who was new in town, who was going where and why.

Given its destination, the Boeing 307 passengers were of particular interest, and the spectacle of the Stranger with Two Two-Ton Suitcases was something new. What could I be carrying?

I staggered on — a reporter in pursuit of a story readily discards all dignity! Success in news usually requires 90 percent attention to detail, 10 percent defiance of all rules. It was imperative that I personally witness my baggage being loaded onto the cargo hold. In Vientiane, no one could be trusted and the city reeked of danger.

It was late August 1969, and though the air war against North Vietnam was on pause, much of Laos was still a free-fire zone for the Air America "secret" war against the communist Pathet Lao, who held sway just a few miles out of town. Adding to the pressure was the awareness that breaking the rules didn't begin to describe this imminent adventure — and my job was certainly at stake. Management had frowned and stalled over this assignment anyway, regarding it as too sensitive politically with the excuse "Look, Vietnam is not Canada's war." But now my baggage was loaded, and on boarding the flight fate took over — though dwelling on it was much too frightening!

There were fewer than thirty of us on the plane, single seats either side of the aisle, so no one talked, nor wanted to. Everyone aboard would rather be a mystery.

Looking down, seeing the Mekong unwind and recede as we climbed, brought back memories of crossing the fast-flowing river from northern Thailand to Laos on a raft with cameraman Phil Pendry, and with all his gear and pockets full of dollars. Insanity, because right then no one in the world knew where we were. It was much the same situation now.

Some ten minutes passed gaining altitude before we heard our pilot's voice over the intercom announcing, "*Madames et m'sr*. We are fortunate. Visibility is good. We should be in Hanoi just before dark, in an hour or so." At that, I felt the adrenalin rush: it was all happening! No North American journalist had been admitted into North Vietnam in recent years. Even though the media thronged Saigon, Hanoi was deemed the heart of darkness, portrayed as a war-hungry rogue society, though there had been no first-hand reports. So the rush was intense. I would be the first allowed in — perhaps.

I had a press visa, for which I'd lobbied for years and which I'd collected only the day before from Hanoi's consular in Vientiane. I was already at the airport terminal when he found me. Anxiously, he thrust at me a telegram from Hanoi dated earlier that day, just eight devastating words: "Serious Red River flooding — regret you cannot come."

Sweating heavily, the consular pronounced one word at a time: "Do-not-get-on-that-flight." Then he left me, standing there, utterly distraught.

My plane (mentally still mine) had already arrived from Phnom Penh, Cambodia, a once-a-week flight supervised by the ICC, International Control Commission, set up by the Geneva Accords in 1954 as a kind of umpire in former Indo-China. In a week there would be another flight; I could try again. No, I couldn't. I couldn't survive a week in Vientiane with nothing to think of but the prospect of failure.

I still had the visa. I could board the flight. But what if Hanoi wouldn't admit me? I could hear Management's condemnation: "You had no valid visa. You kept us in the dark. You've been totally reckless — at huge cost to us."

For years I had pressured them for an okay if I obtained a visa; for years I'd heard their response, "It isn't our war," though it *was*, for the sixties generation everywhere.

The plane was on the tarmac. The story was beseeching my brain. What unique headlines awaited? I'd never find out unless I got on that plane. I knew it was permitted to remain on the ground in Hanoi for only an hour then return to Vientiane. So what were the risks?

On arrival, I could check that my baggage was off and then try to hang back, find a toilet, stall for an hour. I'd have at least a week in Hanoi before the next flight out. At what danger? Hanoi might "arrest" or detain me. Now that would be one helluva story!

First, I destroyed Hanoi's telegram, then somehow I picked up the two bags and staggered out to that beckoning flying machine, itself as improbable as my journey.

CHAPTER TWO
Eye of the Hurricane

I HAD DONE MY curiosity research. The Boeing 307 was the last of ten built, born when I was, some forty years earlier. It was the first pressurized civilian passenger airliner, good for eight thousand feet, which, when I looked out of my window and saw the Truong Son rearing up at us, seemed a pretty close thing. The first test flight of the 307 had crashed. Four others had gone down in various areas of Indo-China, including one that had simply vanished, never found, in this very mountain range on this very weekly flight. The ICC had contracted with a local established French airline to fly the 307s on the risky Phnom Penh–Vientiane–Hanoi route.

The result at this moment was utterly surreal. I might be flying over the Pyrenees. Two beautiful French stewardesses made their way down the aisle. They wore tightly tailored sky-blue costumes, mini-skirts a foot above the knee, hips swaying slightly as, tray in hand, they went seat to seat, murmuring "Candy, *m'sr?*"

I took a last look at the Truong Son, their snow-peaks a thin light in the descending dusk, a scene equally surreal, where unseen millions engaged in perpetual war along mystical mountain trails where the bombing ceased for sure only for this once-a-week ICC flight. How remote this was to the wider world, this saga of the Trail. What an incredible story it was! On this flight to the unknown, my mood veered moment to moment, a yo-yoing of excitement and unease. Exhausted, I fell asleep, woken by a soldier in green fatigues shaking my arm, barking what could only be "Wake up, wake up." Gradually I did so, making sure I was the last passenger off the plane.

Once landed, the Boeing parked right outside a single-storey building that looked like a converted factory. This wasn't the Gia Lam airport

I'd heard of — a place of vaulted ceilings, fine dining, and violinists to serenade the latest batch of French paratroopers about to switch planes for the Waterloo that was Dien Bien Phu. But that was a different war, fifteen years earlier, or arguably the same war, as the U.S. quickly stepped in with military aid and "advisors," then combat troops to support a new Saigon regime.

Perhaps the North Vietnamese found the old Gia Lam too colonial, or perhaps with only the weekly ICC flight and the occasional Soviet flights arriving via Beijing there was no need for anything more than this bleak clearing house, silent except for the shuffling shadows lined up for passport clearance.

I watched as my fellow passengers, each in turn, were met by minders or by friends or embassy chauffeurs, realizing with renewed unease that there was no one here to meet me, no one to vouch for me, and this clearly puzzled the customs man in military uniform who saw my Foreign Ministry visa but saw no one here from the Ministry.

"*Vous Canadien?*"

"*Oui*," and I pointed to the baggage rack where, like old friends, two large suitcases waited. He gestured that I open them, then gaped astonished at the contents. Except for a few clothes and personal items in one case, both were filled with large cans of 400-foot rolls of negative colour film — sixty cans in all.

I was back on the Vientiane tarmac. How had I ever carried them? Then the soldier began tearing the sealing tape off one can and I found my hand grasping his wrist to stop him. He looked at me in disbelief. Did I dare assault the People's Army?

Hurriedly, I pointed to the passport entry, then tapping one can I repeated "*Presse.*" I was in fact both journalist and film documentarian, having pre-arranged to hire a Japanese camera-crew based in Hanoi. All this, of course, was impossible to explain, so I just kept repeating the magic word "*Presse.*" For what seemed ages we just stared at each other until finally he pointed a finger first at me, then at a nearby bench. Like a dog I understood the command: Go, Sit.

So there I sat, smiling only once as I saw the Boeing crew exit the terminal, now completely empty but for the soldier and me. I stared fixedly at him, waiting for some word, but except when making a phone call he totally ignored me. I heard the Boeing take off. Well, at least I'd made it to Hanoi. Did it really matter what happened next?

But increasingly it did, as one hour passed, then a second hour, until suddenly the exit door to the street was flung open and a slim older man of military bearing entered, talked briefly to the duty officer, retrieved my passport, then handed it to me, all without a word. A man whose evening I had clearly ruined! They each picked up a suitcase and led me outside to a jeep, the older man merely gesturing for me to get in.

I guessed he was a senior officer summoned from Hanoi to deal with the oddity in their midst. He drove in silence, using only his parking lights, concentrating on the few feet ahead that he could see, never once looking at me. Clearly any questions, even if understood, would go unanswered.

I had never known a city in such total darkness. Try as I might I could see no landmark, and nothing of that hour-long midnight drive registered on memory. What a bizarre arrival this was! After all, I wasn't being mistreated, just treated as a bloody nuisance! And supposing, instead of a hapless scribe, I had been a spook, some Rambo type. Or, like the number of my Scotland Yard press card, 007 himself. I'd be trained. I'd overpower the driver and take off for the city centre, there to wreak all the fantasies the CIA drooled about for dealing with the "heart of darkness."

In reality, in the pitch black, I had no sense of direction. My spy fantasy lasted mere seconds, shattered by the rutted roads and bouncing jeep and by my protesting empty stomach. I'd gone all day without food and several hours without water, with little prospect of finding either. Torn so many times between delight and dismay, my brain, like my stomach, was running on empty.

My eyes had drooped when suddenly we stopped, and got out. We were at a building with no lights or signs or life. My Vietnamese escort uttered his one word of the night: "L'hotel," and so saying he banged furiously on the shuttered door before unloading my suitcases, then speeding away.

I kept banging to no avail on the hotel door until my hands hurt and I could but laugh at the improbability of it all. Except for me, the street was deserted, the city so quiet it seemed abandoned.

Here I was, the potential secret agent, loose and at large in the heart of Hanoi. But it was all Agent 007 could do to lift the two suitcases to the top step of the hotel. Stretching out on my precious baggage, an unwanted, unexpected foreigner all alone in the Hanoi night, too numb to any longer care what happened next, I was soon obliviously asleep.

The day shift of the Hoa Binh Hotel found me at 5 a.m., curled up in a leaden state. A swarm of diminutive figures, two or three on either side, bore me across the hotel lobby to an office with a large couch.

"*Ogenki desu-ka?*"

"*Hai, genki des, arigato,*" I replied to the two Japanese camera crewmen we'd pre-booked through their Tokyo Head office, which had helped me during my years as Far East correspondent.

This connection certainly helped with the two Vietnamese. In a friendly voice Vu Phuong explained he was an English interpreter. Then he introduced Nguyen Lam of the Foreign Relations committee. Lam had a permanent frown, but courtesy meant that green tea and rice cakes would be served before the scolding could begin. The hot jasmine tea quickly cleared my mind. I might be in trouble, but at least no soldiers had come to drag me off!

Be contrite! I kept silent; protocol dictated that Lam speak first.

Vu translated in staccato bursts: "Did you not get our telegram? You were told not to come.... You were told we face a state of emergency.... There is very serious flooding.... Do you understand you are not expected." A pause, then his voice raised in suspicion. "Why are you here?"

I told them "I am so happy to be here.... I am very sorry your country is facing these new difficulties.... Yes, I read your telegram, but I read it as saying *best* not to come.... But I want to understand your country.... So I came, hoping I can witness and film the history of your times."

At this Lam slightly relaxed. He changed the subject. "This hotel, you see, is just for Vietnamese. Cadres from the countryside. One of them found your passport and called us at the Foreign Ministry."

A pause, then the slightest smile. "Your luggage has been taken to the Thong Nhat Hotel where our Japanese guests live. They will take you there." He stood. "We will consider what you say, but I promise nothing."

The Thong Nhat had a quality of lingering grandeur. Though only three storeys, it sprawled over a city block on one of the gracious boulevards fashioned by the French, which distinguished Hanoi from Saigon. The hotel had a vast lobby with deep, if dilapidated, armchairs scattered around, an enormous mahogany front desk leading to a ballroom-size restaurant that in earlier days had been the favourite gathering place for the colonial diplomatic corps. What captivated was the calm. The Thong Nhat ("reunification") lived in its own sense of time. Assuming I must register, I went first to the front desk, but there was nobody there, nothing except a prominently placed phone. Ah, I should call Canada, but lifting the antique phone I could only get my own voice echoing "Hello, hello?"

"Are there phones in the rooms?" I asked Vu, but it was cameraman Fujii who responded in his chopped-up English.

"Hotel just one phone." He shrugged. "Sometimes works. Not often."

"Room keys?" I asked.

"No keys," Fujii said. "Room ready."

No keys! For decades now, war had raged across South-East Asia, yet here in the very eye of the hurricane things seemed ultra-calm and timeless!

I soon realized the practicality: why waste time on the pursuit of keys? Why then any need for a concierge. Why waste power on elevators? There was no choice but the immense white-marble stairway, its steps so wide and high they seemed, like Everest, to flow upwards and upwards, draining your breath.

Somehow, Fujii-san had managed to haul my leaden suitcases up this marble mountain. He quickly became an inspiration. He was tall for a Japanese, almost six feet but rake thin, and we physically bore a resemblance, though Ryoko Fujii had the elongated face of some *ukiyo-e* samurai. He had the strangest mannerism I'd ever encountered. Somehow, when mentally disengaged, his entire head leaned to his left, as if resting on his shoulder, straightening up only when he talked, which was seldom.

Now, in my room with Vu and the crew, I opened the suitcases to please Fujii, sensing he'd be happy. Fujii loved his craft of photography and for him the sight of so many cans of colour footage was like discovering a treasure trove.

For a few seconds, the open suitcases reduced us all to silence — difficult for sound technician Misao Ishigaki, who was Fujii's opposite, short and constantly chirpy. We all knew that Hanoi had no facility for processing colour film, and so our footage, if the shoot ever happened, could not be physically censored. Events would depend hugely on mutual trust.

"I'd like to go for a long walk, see the city," I told Vu, who'd become our "minder."

Vu said, "I'd have to accompany you and then we'd miss siesta."

I got the message. "Another time, Vu, when we're all rested."

All to myself, the room seemed enormous: a fifteen-foot embossed ceiling, marble-tiled floor and a four-poster bed — the posts serving as a frame for a coverall mosquito net, which gave the bed the look of a ghostly tent. A small side table, two narrow armchairs and giant fan completed the furnishings. Nowhere for clothes, but then I'd brought very little. Indeed, apart from a shaving kit and some medicines, the only essential item I'd decided on was the largest plastic jar I could find, filled with instant coffee mixed with proportionate sugar and powdered milk. Outside each room, I had noticed a large Chinese-made thermos flask full of hot water. What more in the world could one want — shake well and serve!

Unpacking, I checked my few valuables: ten thousand dollars in five-hundred-dollar travel cheques, a new-fangled VISA card which would be useless here, my Nikon gear, my passport with the loose-leaf press visa which might also prove useless, a photo of my wife, Mariko — and in case of serious trouble, the address and phone number of a the highly placed contact who in 1966 had got me a press visa into Communist China at the time of Mao's cultural Revolution, and had now got me into North Vietnam — or maybe into a heap of trouble! I still didn't know which. I kept asking myself, how long must I wait?

Despite the strangest night of my life, despite my extraordinary entry into Hanoi, despite having been here but a few hours, I was the typical Westerner in the East: a figure of incurable impatience.

CHAPTER THREE
Ho Chi Minh's People

MY FIRST RULE VISITING a country new to me is to walk and walk. The conditions and the mood of those at the bottom rung are usually a safe guide to those at the top. And having cabled the Network that I was in Hanoi but filming was delayed, I had time for a lot of walking while waiting on the Foreign Ministry's decision.

The first surprise was the quiet. Though virtually hundreds of cyclists swarmed and weaved through every street, they were strangely soundless, great shoals of unisex figures in black cotton pants and the billowing black silks of the women's *ao dai*. I had expected a carbon copy of Mao's China: loudspeakers relentlessly blaring the Party line, and, replicating the cult of Mao Zedong, giant posters of Ho Chi Minh on every corner. But there was very little of all that.

Hanoi was then a city of half a million people, with the North's population estimated at seventeen million, but now tens of thousands were pouring in from the countryside for the Independence Day celebrations of September 2, an occasion for civic pride. Everywhere I saw water trucks hosing down the streets, people stringing coloured lights from building to building, and, unexpectedly, small Buddha figures with lit-incense sticks and offerings of fruit in store windows or on the carts of street vendors.

We wandered street to street, dodging the concrete cylinders — inventive air-raid shelters — buried in pedestrian pavements every few yards. Hanoi had five hundred thousand of these, or one for every citizen, Vu told me. To demonstrate, he jumped into one of them, pulling a round concrete manhole cover over his crouched body. It was an ingenious defence. I tried but my neck and elephant ears stuck out (the image became a *Globe and Mail* cartoon). But what registered most were the long, orderly queues at food stores and the patient brandishing of worn, multi-stamped ration cards. It reminded me of my childhood in World War Two London, everyone taking turns at the monotony of waiting for a handful or so of essential items, the excitement when the unexpected appeared on store shelves: jam, bananas, sugar, and the rare treat of meat.

For almost five years the bombing had prevented these celebrations, and now this city of a thousand years was making up for lost time. We drifted toward a central gathering place called Reunification Park, where a modest circus was setting up — just a small roundabout but with many giant tents. Clowns strolled among the crowds selling lottery tickets and touting the various attractions. Again, China was my reference point (the perceptions of journalists can so easily mislead!) and I had expected some mind-numbing version of *The East is Red*. Instead, in the first tent there was Marx Brothers-style slapstick: a trapeze artist who kept slipping to howls of laughter. In another tent I watched with several hundred awestruck people jammed together as actors in tenth-century dress on a makeshift stage relieved the fable of three sisters visiting a prince, one of them losing her slipper around midnight.

"It's called 'Tam and Cam,'" explained Vu. "It's our favourite play."

"We've the same story, Vu. We call it 'Cinderella.'"

At this, Vu looked quite annoyed.

From long tradition, the largest crowds converged on Hanoi's central Hoan Kiem Lake, where on a small islet a much earlier legend was being enacted. Threatened by Chinese warlords, the Vietnamese emperor was meditating at the lake when a blindingly bright sword emerged from the waters: a sword to defeat all foes.

"King Arthur and Excalibur," I was about to tell Vu, but then thought better of it.

I was allowed to use my Nikon and began eagerly snapping everyday Hanoi life. I found it reminiscent of London at war's end, when it seemed every British teenager had crowded into the vast freedom of Hyde Park to seek out company. The couple canoeing in the centre of Hoan Kiem Lake I had seen before on the Serpentine; the young adolescents clinging to each other on the next bench were myself and friend.

Except here it wasn't war's end. Tomorrow, or all too soon, these teenagers would separate, the girls to gunnery schools or road repair, the boys — from age seventeen — to the terrors of the Trail, from which in the worst years only one in two would ever return. I had expected North Vietnam to be another Maoist China or another North Korea: despotic, dehumanizing. Instead, it seemed to me that here — years into the war — I was seeing a society significantly different to that which the U.S. (and the media generally) had so long portrayed. Here was a society, albeit Marxist, displaying a motivating, deep-rooted nationalism.

They were fatalistic, these soldier youths, some with tattoos that said *Born in the North to die in the South*. Among them there would be no burning of draft cards, no protests, no reprieve in drugs or set terms of duty; for them the war was forever, a state of life extant long before they were born. Already almost twenty-five years of ceaseless war and no end in sight — nor any particular hurry to end it.

Perhaps that was their greatest strength: their denial of time and their embrace of identity drawn from their history, a people for whom the new foreign ideology was a great leap forward from colonialism, and, anyhow, nationally convenient. After World War Two, Ho Chi Minh, though Marxist, had also turned to America when declaring independence on September 2, 1945.

I wondered how many Americans knew that the Constitution of the Democratic Republic of Vietnam, penned and read by Ho on that date twenty-four years before, began word for word with the pledges of the Constitution of the United States! Or knew that America, to appease its Cold War allies, had reneged on President Franklin D. Roosevelt's pledge never to allow the return of colonialism in Asia.

Later that day, I left the hotel alone, intent on making a courtesy call. Very soon I realized I was being followed, if only because my shadow was so obvious about it. When I stopped and turned to look back, he stopped and just stared at me. Clearly, he wanted me to know I was being followed.

I continued to a narrow side street, recognizing my destination from the one house where a Vietnamese soldier stood outside, legs spread, with a rifle and fixed bayonet. It was pure symbolism and I walked right past him and thumped on the door. This was the office-home of the sole official Canadian representation in Hanoi: two members of the ICC (International Control Commission), then widely perceived as firmly in America's pocket. They both came to the door, seemingly surprised to get any caller. They were in Canadian army uniforms of sergeant and corporal. I explained who I was and that I just wanted to say hello. We sat in a tiny sauna-like living room, wedged into midget chairs, the two ICC men seeming anxious, on guard at the sudden presence of a journalist. But we shared a beer and avoided politics. After a while I told them I'd been scouting the city. There was boating on the lake, there were tens of thousands celebrating, and I added, "There's a circus in town."

At that the corporal could no longer restrain himself. He leapt up. "My God, they got to you, they've bloody well got to you," he bellowed.

I stood up and none of us attempted a handshake. I left them, wondering if they ever left their prison, whether they knew anyone here but each other.

Back at the hotel, my Japanese colleagues were waiting for me, together with the Foreign Relations contact, Lam, on whom I noticed an amused, knowing smile. "I've still no news for you," he said, "but there's an Independence Day reception tonight at the presidential palace and you're all invited — in my company, of course."

"Thank you. Will President Ho Chi Minh be there?"

Lam slowly shook his head before saying, "You will meet others you should know about. No filming, but you may take photos."

Surely, this had to be a breakthrough.

A few hours later I was sipping wine with Defense Minister Vo Nguyen Giap, a one-time history teacher and legendary victor at Dien Bien Phu. I met Le Duan, First Secretary of the Party; Truong Chinh, the Party elder on ideological matters; Van Tien Dung, Commander of the Armed Forces — men whose names were almost totally unknown in Washington or among the American soldiers fighting and dying in South Vietnam. Finally, the key meeting: Prime Minister Pham Van Dong, Hanoi's voice to the outside world. The son of a mandarin, he had helped found the insurrectionist Viet Minh, then spent much of his life in French prisons.

His smile hid those years but his eyes did not. He shook hands, saying, "Ah, the guest who came in the night."

"May I say, Prime Minister, how hopeful I am not to be leaving the same way!"

Pham laughed, then abruptly asked, "Would this documentary you propose be seen in America?" His question made it pretty clear that he was the one deciding what to do with me.

"Certainly, Prime Minister, and worldwide, I believe, depending on what filming is allowed."

He slowly nodded, weighing my polite challenge. Pham was a consummate diplomat; he had negotiated the 1954 Geneva Accords that partitioned Vietnam on the understanding that there would be national elections within two years. Instead, he had now to sustain the deadlocked peace talks in Paris while the North faced some 570,000 U.S. troops shoring up the South in an unresolvable war of attrition. All this could be read in the worn and wary eyes of Pham Van Dong.

Meeting Pham and the key leadership had at the very least provided the material for a special report on the North should I be put on the next plane out. Optimism and pessimism still gripped me moment to moment.

Back at the hotel, only two hours or so after meeting Pham Van Dong, Lam appeared just as we were beginning dinner, saying, "You must come with me now. It is urgent." Now I was sure I was about to be kicked out.

Despite the late hour, the acting head of the Committee for Foreign Relations, Han Viet Tran, had summoned us. The entire committee was there as well as Vu, all very solemn, all wearing black suits and black ties. Tran waited until the obligatory green tea was poured, then without the usual small talk, speaking fluent English, he said, "It is with heavy heart that I tell you our beloved president is gravely ill."

Vu was now crying and Lam seemed on the verge. There was a pause, so I felt I should respond. "This is very sad news and I hope temporary."

We sipped tea, silent for a time. "There is still hope," Tran said, though his voice belied it. "Therefore, the Independence Day celebrations will go ahead. There is to be no announcement. You will not send any cables until we know more. I'm telling you this in strictest confidence so that you and your Japanese colleagues can prepare."

At this Fujii and I both looked at Tran in expectation.

"We have decided," he said, "that since you are here, and since you are here at such an historic time, you may stay. We are a fatalistic people and so we place our trust in your filming. I therefore welcome you to Hanoi."

Ah, the relief! So after all I would not have to inform the Network of the gamble I'd made in coming here without a valid visa (I never did tell them). But of course it was not the time for smiles. "I am grateful for your trust," I said, choking back a hundred questions.

"So, you may now film anywhere within bounds, and Comrade Lam will assist." That meant I'd have a full-time political minder. "And Mr. Maclear, one other thing: do feel free to walk around. Someone will always be looking out for you!"

Back at the hotel, loading the cameras almost ceremoniously, Fujii kept smiling. "They like you, Mike-san, because you took big risks."

"Oh, it's not that — it's because they realize I have no ideological leanings one way or the other and that suits them right now: a journalist with no agenda." Dear Fujii. I'm sure he didn't understand a word of what I'd just said, but even so we had a total affinity. He and sound recordist Ishigaki were as seasoned as any of the many war correspondents I had known. Already they had been three years in Hanoi. At dinner on our first night together they had shown stoicism and humour. Then, and every night, the waitress would hand us the menu scrawled on a scrap of paper. Just two words: *Chicken, Pork*.

That first night Fujii immediately said, "Chicken, Mike-san. Never pork."

Thereafter, every night, with each of us clutching a bottle of Tiger beer, the three of us would sing in chorus to the waitress, "Chicken, chicken, chicken," while I tried to imagine eating nothing else for three long years — and this in the North was the good life!

Perhaps as a precautionary measure, the National Assembly, and all the Party delegates, had convened earlier than usual, a day ahead of Independence Day. But since the entire leadership was present nothing seemed amiss. Ho Chi Minh, ill for many years with heart trouble, was no longer seen in public. What drew attention at the assembly was the sight of our cameras as we filmed unchecked the entire leadership arrayed on the podium.

These were men whose faces, names, and background were still largely unknown to the U.S. military and public, or to the troops in the South, enmeshed in an increasingly demoralizing invisible war. Now, for the first time, foreign media was filming the entire Politburo in what I realized was a show of unity to help weather the coming tragedy of the dying Ho Chi Minh. We were filming candid close-ups of a leadership who called themselves "Council of Equals," and this had held through twenty-five years of war against two superpowers.

But without Ho unity would be harder.

At one point, during a lull in the proceedings, I sat among the delegates for a to-camera explanation of where we were and who was who — and saying how strange it felt!

On Independence Day, huge crowds gathered in Ba Dinh Square, Hanoi's equivalent of Moscow's Red Square and just as vast. At the nearby presidential palace the chanting for "Uncle Ho" never for a moment ceased. The crowd knew, of course, that Ho was not likely to appear, knew that he had never lived at the palace, preferring a small bungalow on the grounds. But very clearly they did not know that Ho was dying.

At this time, we learned that he was on a death watch at a facility outside Hanoi and that the Politburo had agonized over whether to cancel the Independence Day celebrations. But these were the first in five years, possible because of the bombing pause, and to cancel them might have greatly damaged morale. Hanoi had never before been so festive, with coloured lights strung tree to tree around the central lake and street entertainment at every turn. Families had come in force from the countryside, with many thousands reuniting after months and even years of separation. The disastrous floods of recent days had begun to recede, and despite the war raging all around Hanoi, the North had never been so relaxed. In reality, the celebrations were just a day's reprieve before beginning their twenty-fifth year of war.

Twenty-five years! A peasant society that had already fought five times as long as the great powers of World War Two.

What could be learned from such unprecedented defiance? How to capture the nature of an entire people literally born to a cause? Could any outsider ever understand it?

At 4 a.m. September 3, Radio Hanoi announced that Ho Chi Minh was in critical condition. My notes show that he was announced dead at 9:47 a.m. local time. With the national holidays over, the North Vietnamese awoke to a harsh new era, their iconic leader dead and the call to battle ever more relentless.

Perhaps Ho had died days earlier and the need for time out from the war took priority. Of one thing I felt sure: when I was told that I could stay and that we could film, the leadership knew the need to show the outside world that, however intransigent and whoever took over, here was a nation with a human face.

The author during his Tokyo days, 1963. (Photo by Yoshihiko Waku.)

A couple on leave at Hanoi's central lake. Individual freedoms and nationalist traditions were a constant surprise.

The lion dance on every street corner on Independence Day, September 2, 1969.

Traditional cock-fighting draws big crowds.

A vendor sells government lottery tickets.

The face of the enemy!

A swimming pool for war orphans.

Severe rationing took its toll.

An outdoor wrestling match during independence celebrations in 1969.

A line of visiting mourners as Ho Chi Minh lies in state.

Mourners joined in groups so they could afford wreaths to honour
Ho Chi Minh.

First surprise in Hanoi: the 500,000 sidewalk air-raid shelters.

When you hear the sirens, just jump in and pull on the concrete cover.

A nation's grief. Michael Maclear was the only Western witness to this occasion.

All in white: the colour of mourning.

CHAPTER FOUR
The Will of Ho

WHAT I SHALL NEVER forget are the mourners as they left Ba Dinh Hall, where Ho Chi Minh lay in state. Each of them, on leaving the building, appeared totally traumatized. It was as if they were blinded, the men staring straight ahead, seeing nothing, the women putting both hands to their eyes as if to safeguard a vision. Hundreds fainted, collapsing as they emerged; others went into a paroxysm so violent it took several police and medics to restrain them. Hour after hour, mounting and mounting, came screams of grief, not just the wails of people weeping but screams so exhausting that the bereaved could not physically move.

And waiting their turn there was the constant, hypnotic shuffling forward of the queue of mourners that circled inside and outside Ba Dinh Square, a great river of people swelled by innumerable tributaries, queues that flowed from the side streets as hundreds of thousands of peasants, cadres, soldiers, waited in no order of priority. Some would wait a day or more, or travel many days to get here, walking their bicycles so that the saddles could be laden with food for the journey and offerings for the temples. It had been this way for three days now, three days of non-stop filming which I knew would later be the heart of the first documentary on the North since U.S. combat began — a war of which the American public knew very little against an enemy they had never really seen, though in the South it was paradoxically "the living-room war."

With the official funeral scheduled for September 9, Ho would lie in state for another three days, embalmed in an all-glass coffin placed slightly above eye level. For the line of mourners slowly circling the coffin, Ho's profile could only be partially seen, his head deeply resting on a white pillow, his body clothed in light khaki. Gazing at him, it seemed such an inconclusive death. For thirty years, since age twenty-one, he had lived in exile, in France, Russia, then China, and for a quarter century more he had fought two superpowers, vowing "certain victory" yet dying not knowing the outcome. And then, who really was he? What were his beliefs? In secret, it's said, he adhered to ancestor worship, while juggling the opposite dogma of Marxism.

Few people outside the North even knew his actual birth name, Nguyen Sing Cung, which tradition allowed he changed as a youth to Nguyen Tet Thanh and later still to Nguyen Ai Quoc. He had many aliases, Ho Chi Minh ("The Enlightened One") among them, when late in World War Two he and a small band of patriots began organizing in the northern hills for a free Vietnam. Ho was aided then by agents of the OSS — forerunner of the CIA — who needed Ho to help fight the occupying Japanese, specifically to rescue downed American pilots.

On September 2, 1945, when his forces briefly took over Hanoi, Ho Chi Minh wrote and read a Declaration of Independence in part borrowed from that of the United States of America. He had faith in Franklin D. Roosevelt's wartime pledge that America would never support the return of colonialism. But it did, to appease France and to buy British and European support for the widening Cold War. So America looked away as French troops reoccupied their old colony.

Looking at Ho so still, I wondered if part of him had died way back in the mid-forties when the French forces, financed by the United States, drove him back into the hills, and died again in the mid-fifties with the betrayal of the Geneva peace terms.

Emerging into Ba Dinh Square where half a million people waited their turn, I knew I was witnessing a seismic shift in history, a people crying for Ho and crying for themselves, for all the sacrifice past and that yet to come.

Ho's death could only portend a hardening of resolve. He had made history by defeating the French at Dien Bien Phu, the first Asian colonial people to liberate themselves. Now, as they saw it, the enemy and the purpose was the same.

In some ways, Hanoi then was like London after the death of Winston Churchill in 1965, on which I reported for the Network. Then, too, the same queue stretching to infinity, people literally in their millions wanting, *needing*, a last glimpse of an ideal, a summation of their lives that would become their bearings for carrying on. The British, of course, showed minimal emotion, but for them the "blood, sweat, and tears" was long before, whereas Ho had essentially died in battle, commanding his people to fight on.

I needed to cable the Network, but at a dollar a word, each word had to count: "It is both very moving and disturbing to witness the mass grieving. It is more than a people's sorrow — it is the evidence that every single one of Ho Chi Minh's people are readying to fight all the harder."

Back came a cable: "Agencies report serious leadership rivalry. Need update ASAP."

And my terse reply: "Ho always told leadership 'stick together.' They have, they likely will."

Essentially, their cable was saying *Are you missing the story?* In my experience, the Network seemed always to regard any third party news source as more reliable than its correspondent-in-place, a lingering vestige, perhaps, of earlier times when the Network was wholly a news-relay rather than a news-gathering entity — and it was the former which Management still seemed to prefer.

Nearing the official funeral ceremony, the cables became an irritant. Unknown to me, the Network had been auctioning off my services to bigger networks. Daily, the cables became more and more confusing: "We plan to syndicate funeral film worldwide. Advise ASAP how you plan to ship film." Then, "CBS likely to pick up your coverage. Would handle shipment." Then, "NBC now bidding — will advise." Then, "CBS now confirmed. Needs your film shipping plans ASAP."

Perhaps as a seasoned foreign correspondent I should have cared less! But it had been a hard, risky venture getting here. Each cable I opened, I wanted to read: "Terrific, you made it to Hanoi. Good luck..." But the only cables thus far were fixated on how many U.S. dollars they could make from an assignment on which they had wavered throughout!

Yet this was the Big Story. I couldn't risk blowing it because of some petty grudge. Besides, how and where to send out the film had been constantly puzzling me. There were no commercial flights in or out of Hanoi, only the once a week ICC "say your prayers" oldie, and anyhow this didn't coincide with the September 9 official ceremony.

I knew the world would want our film — *if* it were reasonably fresh. So here was the classic conundrum: getting the story was just half the battle, getting it out in this case the harder part, where all would be won or lost.

The logistics for the official ceremony were impossibly tight, and there was no obvious way of getting the film out. Yet it *had* to get out the same day, had to be on air within twenty-four hours. Later than that, well, the film might be interesting and important, but on the news line-up it would be an also-ran. And there'd be no glory at all! And even if we got lucky with a flight that would meet it, what then?

Unlike South Vietnam, which I'd covered innumerable times, North Vietnam had no satellite facilities, no TV, and anyway the Network could not afford satellites at that time. But the American majors certainly could, so how to get the film to CBS? I had an idea, but it needed Tran on side.

It was the eighth and almost the hour of siesta — I must hurry.

I liked Tran — liked his dark humour and directness. "You're sure of the *CBS Evening News*?" he asked.

"Yes, I'm sure *if* they get the film in time. I believe forty million Americans watch it." I knew that was what Hanoi wanted to hear.

"So," Tran said, "we need to know the first plane out after the ceremony."

"It needs to be a 'friendly."

"Russian?" he said automatically.

"No, no. Some plane heading South or West."

"The Russians are the only ones bringing a camera crew. Wouldn't they help?"

"Never trust another TV crew." We laughed. We went down the list of luminaries who'd be attending. Most would be on charter planes from Hong Kong then on the return they'd be boarding connecting flights, so our package could easily go astray.

Cautiously, I said, "I think the best bet is Prince Sihanouk's plane, if he's returning to Phnom Penh."

Tran checked a batch of schedules. "Yes, he is, but ..." he frowned. The Prince and the Politburo were not on the cosiest of terms, with the U.S. then "secretly" bombing NV camps inside the Cambodian border and Sihanouk keeping quiet about it.

"You'd have very little time. The funeral ceremony starts at 7 a.m. and lasts forty minutes, then after a brief rest and buffet the foreign guests all start leaving. Sihanouk is scheduled out at noon."

"We have to arrange it with Sihanouk's pilot on arrival here."

"Alright, you may do that."

"Not me, Mr. Tran. Why would they do me such a favour?" Now came the moment I had been leading to. "The request has to come from your Foreign Office, or better still, higher."

Tran looked aghast. So I smiled. "Forty million Americans, and my network is syndicating the film worldwide. Hundreds of millions may see it." He was silent, our thoughts the same: so many millions the world over who'd never seen any news, who had almost zero knowledge of North Vietnam.

"I will do my best," Tran said firmly. I went directly to the post office and in cable-ese informed my many bosses: "Advise CBS efforting Sihanouk's plane ex Hanoi–Phnom Penh 1500 hours 9th pilot will be pigeon."

At dinner that night the waitress brought over a bottle of Russian vodka with a gift card. The cover was of a bird in flight and the message inside said, "Pigeon agrees. To success — Tran."

Hanoi must have been arm-twisting Phnom Penh big time. Then Tran's message struck me: the pigeon bit. They were reading my cables and he was letting me know it, though I'd expected as much.

The meal was chicken — I think, for the vodka disguised it. "*Kampei*, Fujii-san, Ishigaki-san." Only twelve hours to go!

At breakfast, 5 a.m. on the ninth, Tran came personally to the Thong Nhat and immediately we thought that after all we were not to film. But Tran was affable enough. "You're leaving for the southern provinces early tomorrow morning. You'll be gone at least three or four weeks with permission to film the bombing aftermath. You must inform your network because it will be, how you say? No picnic. We must prepare. Now."

"We'll need two jeeps."

"Yes, two jeeps, eight people."

"Why eight?"

Tran explained: two drivers, our English interpreter, a Japanese interpreter as backup, our crew of three, and the coordinator-minder, Lam.

"This evening be sure you have everything you'll need. Start with mosquito nets. Now," Tran smiled, "we must work out the cost. You must pay in U.S. dollars."

The jeeps were U.S. $100 a day each, gasoline $50 a day per jeep, the per diems (including water and soft drinks) a modest $20 per person, times however many days. It was already over $10,000 with the hotel and incidentals still to pay. I'd be cleaned out. The Network would have to wire more funds. Management would foam.

But I sensed this story was bigger even than the death of Ho.

I fetched my book of travel cheques, signed every one of twenty $500 notes and gave them to Tran, who in turn handed us bundles of brand new, low-denomination Dong — worthless everywhere else in the world. Tran smiled. "Look after each other and you'll be alright."

We were up at 4 a.m. and had a hurried breakfast, an hour to load the gear, get through the crowds, and get to our reserved seats by the 5 a.m. deadline, amazed to find we were front-row, thanks doubtless to CBS, though of course they wouldn't know it. Then a long insanity of sitting there in suit and tie as the temperature rose to 107 degrees by 7 a.m., when the ceremonies began.

At least half a million people filled Ba Dinh Square. Fujii stood on his seat to get a better sense of this sea of white, the colour of mourning. All the men wore white shirts, the women silk white *ao dai*, and even the military bands wore special white uniforms and white hats. We were free to move among them. Lam and Vu had kept their distance; at no time were we stopped in our filming. Every few seconds in the intense heat, even among the ranks of soldiers, someone would faint, and alert teams of medics would carry them off. On the grandstand facing the vast crowd, Prime Minister Pham Van Dong, a handkerchief to his eyes, was crying profusely.

On either side of him the two principal guests, Soviet Premier Alexei Kosygin and China's Vice Premier Li Xiannian, kept dabbing their foreheads, never once glancing at each other. So much for all the fear of monolithic Communism! It was visually a perfect capsule of the Sino-Soviet drift.

Fujii and I moved in lock-step. I noted every shot he took, noted the change of mood. The sobbing now was gentler than in previous days, just the quiet tears of closure. I began writing the script in my head. I needed to memorize some five minutes of copy, needed to match facts and film, needed to emphasize what was politically meaningful and what was simply soulful, like the hysteria at Ho's lying in state which the outside world had yet to see. I'd have maybe five minutes back at the hotel to type a script then voice it, then stampede to the airport in search of our pigeon.

As First Secretary of the Party ("first among equals"), Le Duan began reading Ho Chi Minh's last written words, some functionary presented me with an English-language copy of Ho's "Will." It wasn't the words that were so significant but the fact that they were in English. I looked around. No one else in that crowd, nor among the foreign delegations that had flown in, had English as a first language. As for the media, aside from a Russian television crew and the Hanoi bureaux managers of Nihon Denpa News and Agence France-Presse, I was the only foreign correspondent there.

But that "Will" in English, so lovingly designed, certainly hadn't been printed just for me! So at some stage in the arrangements for Ho's death, Hanoi had hoped and prepared for an important contingent of English-speaking guests — Americans! The document in my hand seemed to speak. Everything fit. It was an open secret that the previous May, shortly before Ho had written his "Will" with its exhortation to "fight on," Henry Kissinger, then President Nixon's secret envoy at the Paris peace talks, had been meeting there with his North Vietnamese counterpart, Le Duc Tho.

It would later emerge that a political settlement involving early release of prisoners and a twelve-month phased withdrawal of troops had been agreed to in principle, but the Saigon government refused to accept the interim presence in the South of NV troops and so the deal collapsed. Had it been endorsed, then for sure American officials and the American media would be reading Ho's "Will" as I was then!

(In writing this book, I return again and again to the University of Toronto's Robarts Library, whose Media Commons retains my Vietnam archives.

In a folder marked "Ho's funeral" I've rediscovered his "Will" — and the revelation it had for me originally remains as intense now. It is a glimpse of what might have been: a war that but for failed diplomacy might have ended that year I first went to the North, 1969. In its English version it is a rare document, six pages of high-quality, glossy paper with the front title "WILL of President Ho Chi Minh." It contains a reproduction and translation of Ho's last handwritten thoughts, dated May 10, 1969, after he had suffered two heart attacks. The "Will" is his last exhortation to his people to fight on, then "victory is an absolute certainty." The war, he writes, "may drag on" but finally "we will build our country ten times more beautiful." At the time he wrote those words, the framework for a peace settlement had evidently collapsed, yet the final settlement would be little different except that it would "drag on" for four more years of all-out war — unwinnable combat for both sides.

Ho's "Will" is a testament to how little superiority of arms matters in guerrilla warfare, a testament to a people's readiness — be it understandable or not — to die for a cause. The "Will" was only so many words on paper, but like Baghdad or Kabul today, the evidence, the warning was there those many decades ago on the streets of Hanoi.)

I knew that my lone English copy of Ho's "Will" was a story in itself: so much that it didn't tell, all the backroom political schemes and dreams. What was known and what was conjecture was far too complex to explain in the report I now had to prepare. The foremost secret of getting your report on air was to provide options, a script that could run several minutes or just a minute if that's all the network news that night had room for. It meant avoiding anything that required too much explanation or mental attention. Such is television news!

Everything that was lost in Paris, the years of agony still to be faced because no side could compromise, above all the determination of this strange guerrilla society, I could only convey in my report by quoting Ho, "The resistance war may drag out ... but we fight till total victory."

Now came an acid test. "Ten minutes, Mike-san." Ishigaki flashed both hands, giving me a ten, the time he figured we had left to make it to the airport and find our pigeon. I still had to write the script and then voice it on audio tape. I had the script typed in five minutes, but now we couldn't find anywhere to voice it.

Everywhere, the hotel echoed with the chatter of so many guests returning all at once from the funeral. "Noise much," Ishigaki kept saying as we went from my room to his to Fujii's, where finally I was able to record the script in the quiet of the toilet. I hoped it wasn't symbolic!

At six the next morning we set out in two overcrowded, overladen, and certainly, at $100 a day each, overpriced Russian-built "jeeps" in which springs must have cost extra. Even driving in Hanoi we were like some puppet show, heads bouncing and colliding. I was upset anyway at not knowing whether our pigeon had been met at Phnom Penh. Any cable from the Network or CBS would take a day more to reach Hanoi and pass the censors, and we would now be beyond contact for weeks.

After the high of making it to Hanoi and gaining exclusivity to a major news event, the sudden plunge into media darkness was indescribably depressing. Where we were heading there'd be no communication except by runner. We were travelling back a century or so! But equally upsetting was the fact that Vu wasn't with us, replaced by a different interpreter, Ba Nguyen Vien, whose greeting was a glare.

"Where's Vu?"

"He's resting. Why do you ask? It isn't your business."

You couldn't get a more hostile beginning than that. We'd entered Ba Dinh Square, now strangely deserted, and then further on stopped at a building I knew to be the Foreign Ministry.

Vien snapped at me, "You are to see the press censor."

Moments later I was sipping unwanted tea as a stone-faced official shuffled some file on his desk then handed me a sheet of paper. Vien interpreted. "Where did you get this information?"

In case our film went astray, as backup I'd cabled the Network some colour passages from my script. Now I read, "Someday Ho Chi Minh, it's understood, will be enshrined here in a Leninesque mausoleum. But while the war continues his place of entombment will not be revealed." As Tran had obliquely warned me, perhaps to prepare me, my cables were being read. I took the offensive. "Are you saying this information is incorrect?"

"I'm asking where you got it."

I fudged, "My cable says 'It's understood.'"

"It should be understood that certain information is classified."

"I'm not Vietnamese. I can't read or speak Vietnamese, so I can have no idea what might be classified." I paused. This situation had to be ended. "You failed to make me aware of censorship. So any breach is your fault."

His eyes widened in astonishment. I followed up with, "What is your authority for ordering me here this morning?"

We'd reached stalemate. We both stood and he quietly said, "I regret this misunderstanding." I nodded and walked out, without even waiting for Vien, suspecting that he was my punishment for that cabled information. It was a troubled start to what was certain to be a punishing journey.

CHAPTER FIVE
Into the Wasteland

LEAVING THE OUTER REACHES of Hanoi there was the déjà vu look of a thousand such anonymous towns in Asia: the seemingly endless open-air market with its orchestral sound of wandering goats and chickens, the patient, laden crowds at the bus terminal where the wanted bus might or might not come that day, the shoals of cyclists as programmed as worker bees, the rail crossing where the barrier never seemed to lift, and everywhere the shabby low-rise buildings so dust-covered as to be unnoticeable. The traveller saw it all and saw nothing, until abruptly we'd left Hanoi behind and there really was nothing to see. The "highway" had become a rutted dirt road hardly wider than our jeeps, the market throng had become an occasional roadside vendor, and the cyclists seen at a distance were strangely misshapen, like caravans of humped camels.

Gradually, the silhouettes of urban life, anything of brick and mortar, thinned out then faded to black — the black of the floodwater lapping close to the roadside, the black of the low-hanging clouds reflecting the black of our mood.

We were as organized as possible. It was agreed that Fujii and I would ride in the lead jeep with Vien, our English interpreter, up front with the driver, so that he could quickly translate "Stop" whenever I said it. Lam, our coordinator and "minder," was in the second jeep with Ishigaki and the Japanese-language interpreter. If we stopped to film and Lam said "No," we would accept that as final.

Our destination was the 18th Parallel, four hundred kilometres from Hanoi — half a day's drive on Western roads. But so great was the bombing devastation, we were allowing two weeks to get there, involving numerous side-trips, and a week or so to return. We would follow Highway 1 as shown on our pre-war maps, but each day there would be difficult unmapped side journeys in search of somewhere to eat and sleep.

Word had gone ahead: every fifty miles or so district cadres would be waiting to guide us to some rest place and the day's main meal. The second jeep bore provisions — rice, chicken broth, dried fruit, bottled water — which would be strictly rationed over an estimated thirty days. The lead jeep held all the precious camera gear, and keeping it safe slowed us even more. On one side of the road, to the east, there was flooding for miles ahead. To our right, the patterned rice-paddies stretched to the horizon. If either jeep was to ditch, we'd be in deep water, figuratively and literally. So we'd agreed on a speed of no more than ten miles an hour — *if* that was possible.

Even with the relative road comfort of the first ten miles Fujii and I said not a word. We were already in considerable discomfort: two gaunt figures jammed together in the rear, heads brushing the low canvas roof, Fujii clutching his Auricon camera, ready to instantly begin filming, awaiting my cry of "Stop," which never came because those first few miles were a desert of water with the known world receding in a series of bouncing jolts mocking us in the jeep's wobbling rear-view mirror.

I'd been carefully eyeing the odometer. After ten miles there was no discernible landmark in any direction. And with nothing to see there was nothing to film! Silent tension gripped us all. Despite the "pause" after four and a half years of Rolling Thunder, offshore U.S. carrier-based Skyhawks were everywhere, maintaining reconnaissance, and a lone two-jeep convoy had to be a tempting target!

And then it happened. In the same instant that we heard the jet's thunderclap, our driver violently braked. And Vien, our hostile minder, began furiously shaking his fist at the sky before turning to glare at me, though the Skyhawk had done no more than scare us. Unlike Vu, my first minder after my arrival in Hanoi, Vien had no time for any foreigner, not least the Japanese who had occupied Vietnam during World War Two.

We all got out to stretch, Lam offering us the favourite cigarettes of the North called "Dien Bien Phu." Everyone constantly smoked.

Now, dissolving the tension, came the cheerful chatter of young women. Driving on, it was an unexpected sight: some twenty young women forming a human chain, passing buckets of earth from one to the other, with the woman at the head of the line constantly emptying the buckets into a gaping pothole at the side of the road.

There was a sensuous rhythm to it, the women swaying slightly, laughing, joking, their shouldered rifles smothered under long black hair and the traditional conical hats resting on their backs — incredibly grace-ful women all alike in their standard black cotton tunics and trousers. Where the line began, a few more young women were pounding the ridge of an old bomb crater with their rifle butts to create the supply of healing earth. And then, the pothole filled, a few of them formed a circle, almost musically stomping down the earth. They were aware of our camera, and there was much giggling and coy glances. Then they were gone, so silently they now seemed imaginary. I noticed that Fujii had the same huge grin as me. We had just filmed something quite unique, a tableau of how the North held out, due in large part to its women.

The sudden filming had rejuvenated our mood. How wonderful to be in strange lands, each day on the good days rich with insight, rich with images that we knew would long outlive us.

The glow of a good day's shoot, the zigzag of the mind mentally editing the footage as we filmed it, the knowledge of the profound influence that a few frames of film can have, this was why we were here. It's the good days that live on — the bad days, the grindingly routine assignments that were the larger part of the job, were too numerous to remember!

As much as the unknown ahead of us was the tension with the Network. I knew my film on North Vietnam, even though exclusive, would be seen by management as sensitive, likely to bring unwanted attention, film it would feel obliged to run but would sooner not, and in any argu-ment over the facts the Network would likely not be at my side. Perhaps most network news organizations were much the same, nervous when confronting government in time of war, muffled by the flouting of a flag.

So often during the journey south I'd see the wasteland come alive, mostly units of young women mending the stricken southern provinces. They had done so, Lam explained, throughout the years of bombing, emerging at night to tend the wounded, repair the roads, harvest the rice. Their existence hadn't changed with the bombing cessation. They lived on the job, rested when they could in hideouts only they knew, keeping only the company of other women, each unit responsible for a section of Highway 1 and its environs. What I'd seen was just a glimpse of a vast, historically unique all-women resistance: the soldiers of the home front.

We drove on, but soon I shouted "Stop." Vien ignored me and I watched as a strange caravan of bicycles slipped past our jeep like a vision lost. But there was a larger caravan immediately ahead. "Stop!" I shook Vien's shoulder and this time he instructed the driver. Scrambling out, I knelt by the roadside, gesturing to Fujii to film from that angle.

In seconds the caravan was upon us, soundless except for the gasp of old men fighting for breath. Each pushed a load that must have been at least a hundred kilos, strapped to a widened saddle, rising like a hump behind the old men bent over the handlebars: human camels in their thousands who'd replaced most vehicular traffic. This was the task of men unfit for the front, men in their fifties and sixties, men who were surely shortening their lives with each mile they pushed with labouring breath.

This, too, was a glimpse of the guerrilla nation that North Vietnam had become, a society grimly determined while knowing the price.

The caravan of old men paid no attention to us. Where they had come from, where they were going, I'd never know. I wanted to shout at them, "You are part of the record — you exist on our film." Filming them had lasted some two minutes, the kind of film gem I had faced every obstacle to get, for which I'd come from the other side of the globe and almost missed this treasure. I was furious with Vien. I grabbed his arm. "Call Lam, tell him you're no help to me. Tell him in the future we'll stop when I say stop. Tell him, damn you."

We'd come twenty-five miles, with the day's target, Phu Ly, ten miles further on, but the road was so pitted with bomb craters that the next five miles were the worst yet, taking a bone-jarring hour. And then there was a river to cross — a river with no bridge. On the far side another bicycle caravan waited. How was anyone to get across? It had to mean another film gem, but this time Lam, the senior minder, raised his hand palm down, the sign for "No."

Any kind of communications — rail or road junctures, river crossings — were militarily sensitive and could not be filmed. Those were the terms agreed to. The alternative was to film — and learn — nothing.

So we could only watch, sitting on the river bank, smoking, seeing the floating patches of reeds coming towards us, yet not seeing until awareness dawned. I looked at Lam pleadingly but he shook his head. The floating reeds, having reached our crossing point, seemed to levitate maybe three feet higher than the river, and then we could see the camouflaged raft and on either side six noticeably muscular young women, arms upright holding the raft aloft, their mouths still biting on sections of reeds they used as air-pipes. Like aquatic performers they slowly rotated the heavy log raft until it could be slotted into metal clasps dug into both sides of the river.

It was a highly stylized act and within minutes we had our bridge. But on the other side I called Lam, showing him on the map a narrow side road a little further on, leading directly to the city of Nam Dinh. "That's our last stop before returning to Hanoi in a few weeks," he said.

"It's very near. I'd really like to see it now."

He shook his head. "There would be no one there to meet us."

Exactly, I thought. As the only city in the southern provinces, Nam Dinh's condition might speak to whatever else lay ahead. "Mr. Lam, I need to say I chose freely the places we visit."

He surprised me with a quick "Very well."

So now we turned east, toward the coast, finding the route well repaired, and soon Fujii nudged me. "City, Mike-san."

Though some two miles distant, on the flat plain the outline of buildings seemed quite normal but dark under a now-black sky. Then a new sight: every few hundred yards groups of young boys, none older than twelve, were repairing the road even now in the pounding rain. We sped by, hoping for shelter somewhere in the city, but suddenly the road came to an end, blocked by a vast pile of rubble.

For some twenty minutes we made our way on foot between unrecognizable streets of ruined buildings, stumbling, at times falling on the mounds of jagged debris. Finally, drenched, decidedly odd in our see-though knee-length plastic attire with matching hats, we came to a totally flattened area, perhaps once a city square. Here, a crude memorial painted on shattered planks portrayed a dive-bomber hovering over piles of dead, with the date 14-4-1966.

But clearly much of this devastation was the work of B-52 "carpet" bombing, for some demolished buildings, mostly two storeys, were evenly ruined for a quarter mile or so, while others surrounding the area still stood but with roofs, windows, floors ripped apart by the blast.

Our French-era map identified Nam Dinh as a city of ninety thousand people with a prized textile centre and a major harbour which I could not get near, though it surely had been gutted. I could only comment on what I saw while walking slowly amid the rubble in a 180-degree panorama so that the camera also saw everything I described. For some minutes it all seemed totally lifeless. Then, nearing a long row of two-storey buildings, to my astonishment every shattered window space, one atop another as far as I could see, slowly began to fill with the children of Nam Dinh.

There they silently stood, not a murmur, looking down at us, six or more crowding each window, kindergarten children mostly but here and there a mother holding her infant. Moving gradually toward them was a tall alien figure hidden in hooded plastic, now frantically snapping photos. I must have seemed to them a spectre of their suffering. But as I neared they still did not move; only as Fujii and I found a way into the ruins did they shrink back from us, but without a cry, without a word. Like the carriages of a train, we could now walk from one low-rise building into another, and I counted at least a hundred children amid these corridors of hell, children who just stared and stared as if into an unending past.

The bombing of the city by U.S. navy pilots had been ceaseless, sometimes twice a day, through 1965, according to an old woman chaperone Lam brought over to us. I took notes. After a brief bombing pause to encourage peace talks, Lyndon Johnson's Rolling Thunder resumed at Nam Dinh without any warning on April 14, 1966, and then the city's population and all industry were totally evacuated to the forested Truong Son hideouts. Casualties? The old woman just shrugged.

I gestured to Fujii and Lam to move outside since the rain had now stopped and we needed light for our filming. But first I beckoned the children to follow, saying to them over and over, "Ca-na-da." Soon, scores of ragged kids, some with a hint of a smile, were lining up against a background of ruins extending as far as we could see. Some instinct had led me here to this scene of carnage of which the outside world, in particular the American public and media, had been kept ignorant for almost five years. And these children? I had not been expected here, so no filming could be more authentic.

"Mr. Lam, these buildings are totally uninhabitable. So what are all these children doing here?"

He and the old woman chatted for a few moments. "They are on a summer camp outing, just for the day," Lam said.

"A camp outing? Be serious! Why are they here?"

He paused. "They are here to learn. They are here to remember. One day they too must join the fight."

We got to Phu Ly, our officially scheduled destination, around 2 p.m., well past siesta time, and I could see that our unfriendly interpreter, Vien, was edgy. For all of us, it was physical pleasure to get out of our ancient Soviet oven, despite the brutal humidity.

Vien was the first out and I heard someone greeting him: a cadre who'd been waiting hours for us. He would direct us toward an overnight resting place, another hour and a half drive toward the Western hills. At that Vien turned to me, tapped his watch, and snapped, "That's it for today."

"No, it isn't. I haven't come to Vietnam to sleep." I looked at the rubble of Phu Ly all around us, and gestured. "This is more important than siesta."

"Tomorrow," Vien said. "Tomorrow we come back this way."

"I don't trust in tomorrow." God, I'd just uttered my whole life's philosophy, fittingly in a landscape of no tomorrows.

Where we'd stopped there was a small, curved headstone that seemed very old. *Phu Ly* was all it said. All around, nothing. I knew from our old maps that Phu Ly had been an important rail junction, with a population of twelve thousand scattered among dozens of villages. On the map, the rail line branched eastward to Nam Dinh, the city we'd just left, and continued south to Ninh Binh and Thanh Hoa, our destination for tomorrow. Objectively, Phu Ly would have been a convenient staging post for men and supplies headed for the Ho Chi Minh Trail, the mountain range directly to the west, and thus a legitimate military target — if anything was legitimate in this undeclared war. Even so, it had been pounded into dust. The inhabitants would have had no warning of the rain of bombs. Squadrons of B-52s flying six miles high, unseen and unheard, would systematically obliterate sections of their target, day after day. Unlike Hanoi, which was ringed with Soviet SAM missiles, here in the rural areas there was no adequate defense. Yet I could not for certain verify that the flattened rubble shown to us as Phu Ly was indeed Phu Ly. However, going by the maps and the mileage from Hanoi, we were exactly where Phu Ly should have been.

We were seeing what no foreigners had ever seen, a wasteland without life. Walking here I could find no evidence of Phu Ly's prior life, no visible wreckage except two twisted rail lines poking a foot or so above the earth, like a hopeless plea. For the Japanese camera crew this was also all new — the furthest they had been from Hanoi during the three years they had been based there. Fujii was as anxious as me to film, in the old saying, anything that moved. But here nothing moved, nothing lived.

He could only film me walking and looking, but that kind of film would not be very convincing. I was baffled. No bombing could be so totally surgical as to wipe out all traces of former life. My guess was that over the years, monsoon and floods had added layers of earth to bury Phu Ly. As for the headstone where our jeeps had stopped, it had likely been planted after the recent bombing pause, not to say *Phu Ly* but to say *Here lies Phu Ly*.

Perhaps the showdown with Vien was inevitable, but still it was ugly. We'd arrived at our rest place for the night, a cluster of makeshift huts mercifully shaded under a high canopy of branches. For at least the last mile or so our path had been hidden under ancient intertwined trees, a bower both peaceful and protective. It was already 4 p.m. and in an hour or so the sun's arc would alter; the moment was precious. Almost immediately I called Vien to tell Lam we were doubling back. We'd walk a quarter mile and then, on the return, we'd slowly film this scenic symbolism of continuance!

I told Vien if he was tired, fine, we didn't really need him. He exploded. "You are not a good comrade, you care nothing for the workers. You are swine."

"I'm not anyone's comrade, Vien. I'm a journalist. Independent, you understand?"

Then, as Fujii and Ishigaki moved supportively close to me, Vien spat at us just as Lam, hearing the shouting, arrived, horrified. Vien kept repeating, "Capitalist swine — you are here to exploit us."

"No, not to exploit, to explain — here to explain your country."

"My poor country, my poor country." Vien was sobbing now, his chest heaving, a figure of exhaustion.

"Vien, I'm sorry —"

But now he turned away, and each of us, tired and distraught, retreated to our respective huts. I had to bend to enter mine, a straw roof with bamboo walls on three sides and no door. Otherwise, just a wood plank "bed" wedged to one wall and under it a tin pan in case of need in the night. Each of us had brought the essential mosquito net, which I now taped to the straw roof, then rolling up my trousers as a pillow I submitted to the agony of the plank and to the torture of the disaster I feared I had wrought. Couldn't I have been more caring for Vien? How selfish had I been; must the story always come first? Had I needlessly brought anger into this sanctuary? So now, what were the odds? In the worst scenario, absolutely no one in my world knew where I was or what might become of me! At best, I had blown the whole venture and would now be kicked out. Vividly, I could hear the derision of the Network and the end of this treasured life as a foreign correspondent.

I thought of that film sequence I'd wanted: those trees that led to the Trail and maybe to one Vietnam one day. Now the sequence was lost to the dusk and in the morning the sun would be low and fierce. I was right, I told myself: Never trust in tomorrow. So then why even think about tomorrow! On that wry note I fell asleep.

CHAPTER SIX
Civilization Lost

AT SIX, OUR DELAYED siesta over, we were each given a bucket of well water to wash down, and we each took reluctant turn at the toilet gouged from the ground some fifty feet behind the huts. "Where's Vien?" I asked Fujii.

"Gone."

"Gone? Gone where?"

It needed both our Vietnamese and Japanese interpreters to explain the situation. Lam had sent Vien back to Hanoi in the second jeep with a letter to the Committee for Foreign Relations "seeking instructions." They had left two hours ago. Poor Vien — a full day condemned to that jeep.

Then I realized it would be late tomorrow before we heard our fate. "Seeking instructions" was not exactly a recommendation for carrying on, more a "You figure out this mess." I just hoped the pragmatic Tran would be the one handling matters. Whatever the outcome, Fujii would have to report to his home office in Tokyo, but this had its positive side. The Japanese crew had high-level contacts in Hanoi. Nothing severe would happen to them and perhaps that protected me.

We ate our meal of brittle rice and sweet mini green bananas in almost total silence, after which Lam fetched us to meet our host, Nguyen Diem Ca, senior cadre of Nam Ha province. We sat in a circle on the floor of another bamboo-thatched hut with a large French-era map spread out between us. I felt encouraged at this obviously staged session — why bother with it if they were really unforgivably angry! After the obligatory green tea, I took copious notes: Ca told us Nam Ha province had a population of 1.7 million, or a quarter of that of all the southern provinces.

First air strikes started in May 1965, thereafter an average of two air raids a day for 1,700 days up to the current pause.

Phu Ly, Ca said, had been a cluster of some forty hamlets each with about sixty families of five or more persons. Casualties? Ca was silent for a while. He had lost many relatives in the bombing and for some moments his eyes closed in memory.

"At first very high. Children and old people. But now 80 percent evacuated, as well as their industry."

"Why evacuate them now?"

At this Ca stood to leave, saying with certainty, "Because the bombers will come again."

At the hut's open doorway, framed against the dark, Ca turned to us, his words emphatic. They would prevail. Home was the caves where their ancestors had lived when fighting the French, and before that when fighting the rapacious warlords of China, and before them fighting the Mongols. So it had been for two thousand years.

A pause, then "America will tire," he said as he embraced the night.

Lam, our minder, began tracing the route on the map right to the partition line at the 17th Parallel, saying "I wish you could go here. Then you would know our spirit." Here was a guerrilla stronghold like no other, "the unseen city" of Vinh Linh, existing fifty feet or more underground, where, Lam said, seventy thousand people lived in a vast grid of connecting tunnels to guard the partitioned border from infiltration.

Perhaps I looked skeptical because Lam repeated "Seventy thousand." It seemed impossible, and pre-empting my question he said, "You can't go there — it's military only and very dangerous." He looked from me to Fujii, saying, "The bombing there continues. So far twenty of our military cameramen have been killed while filming the air attacks."

Lam was the perfect "minder" — a mind reader! "In Hanoi we can show you the film of Vinh Linh taken by the People's Army, even the life underground."

He described that life as "apocalyptic normalcy" where the sacrificial thousands had only the most essential facilities, where families had their own quarters and where, for a few risky minutes at a time, the newborn were gradually exposed to sunlight by being placed in cribs hoisted up vertical tunnels.

I asked Lam if he had seen the other towns on our planned route.

"No, none of us have. But today you have seen how life goes on."

At my hut, in the ebony dark, my mosquito net hung so low it made breathing harder. Stretched on the plank, with minimal room to move, legs and arms became painfully cramped, preventing much sleep. Only the slight breeze from the open doorway fed morale. Life might go on but it begged extraordinary self-control. Long into the night, I listened inescapably to a chorus of snorts and grunts of my various fellow creatures around my doorway and to the ceaseless chirping of cicadas trying to harmonize existence.

I tried to imagine 1,700 nights hiding in the dark from the rain of bombs. The worst of the London blitz, as I remembered it, lasted perhaps five hundred nights. And here, in Ca's words, the bombers could return any time. *Would* return. Of course, the North had to keep sounding the alarm. There was still the war in the South to wage, and only the most rigid discipline and sacrifice could sustain it. I could never verify Ca's account. I could only rely on what our film would show — if ever this strangest of journeys was to continue. At that moment the only indisputable fact was the agony of the plank and the likely wrath of Hanoi — and perhaps worse, the wrath of the Network.

But why think of tomorrow? Listen only to the cicadas and you'll sleep!

A pail of water left at my doorway brought the freshness of a new day. First, I carefully folded my mosquito net. While travelling in wartime Vietnam it was the most precious possession. Then I ran for a few minutes, circling round and round our huts, trying to shake away the aches of the plank! After that I let the well water pour over my head and when Fujii showed up, jokingly pointing his camera at me, I spontaneously began a recorded "take" explaining, as I bathed, how so many generations in the North had adapted to this life. This war, I said, could be summarized in one word: cause. That is, which side truly believed in its cause, whatever the cost.

We tried to prolong breakfast, knowing it would be a long day, but the rice soup went all too fast. Would we hear from Hanoi today or would there be another night on the dreaded plank? We tried filming our huts, more as a memento, but it was silly; the huts were relative luxury in these parts, and, besides, seen through the viewfinder the effect was quite tranquil, our circle of huts idyllic. It's not that the camera lies — almost the reverse. So often it sees a better side to things than does the human eye! By late morning, with the temperature at 110 degrees, numbing the brain, we made our way toward the entrance path where the high trees offered shade and serenity. I saw Lam wave us off, as if saying there were no military secrets there.

But indeed there were: the protective trees emblematic of many thousands of hideaways like this that had outlasted every enemy.

It was some sense of this that I had wanted to film before the confrontation with Vien, but now the idea seemed far too ethereal. Instead, we spread out between bulging tree roots and allowed ourselves an early siesta.

Perhaps it was the remoteness or the geographic oddity of the two places, but when we awoke I found myself babbling about a long-ago trek to the Himalayas in search of the Dalai Lama after he had fled Tibet. I found him at a one-time British hill-station named Mussorie, on a splendid plateau ten thousand feet up. He agreed to an interview. His Holiness was then only twenty-four and at twenty-nine I could be a bit uppity. Finally, I asked him — since I had always wondered — "What is the meaning of life?"

For quite a long time the young God on Earth debated with his assembly of apostles, then gravely replied, "Life is a fountain." As a news item it wasn't very helpful, but nevertheless memorable — and, I felt, in my present circumstances, applicable. I tried to explain to my yawning Japanese audience how our protective wall of trees was also as renewable as the water of a fountain. But clearly they had not understood more than a word or two, and in truth I also had no sure idea what His Holiness meant. But then I saw Fujii's smile again some two hours earlier as he filmed me washing away the night at our hideaway's life-giving well.

Life is a fountain.

Life is a pail of water.

*   *   *

All three of us were half asleep again when the screech of a jeep and the shout of a familiar voice awoke us, a happy voice: "Great news — I am with you!"

"Vu! You're with us the whole trip?"

"Yes, yes. And the Committee sends its greetings and this —" He thrust at us two bottles of vodka as well as a batch of cables. We were cheering so loud it brought Lam running. Vu kept saying "I'm happy, I'm happy" as we hugged one another in sheer relief.

Now it seemed fated that our remarkable journey was to continue. I was careful to keep the cables, which explained the situation. Home office extended its congratulations on my entering the North, the tone unusually friendly, perhaps because — as more cables explained — the American majors were bidding for U.S. rights to anything we filmed. Our footage of Ho Chi Minh's death had been syndicated to seventy countries. My report narrated in a hotel toilet was a seven-minute lead on *CBS Evening News with Walter Cronkite*. It was this American audience that Prime Minister Pham Van Dong had asked about, and now here, very clearly, was the answer. And of course Hanoi was reading all cables. But right then I was glad they were, though there was one cable from a colleague that hurt. "You lucky bastard you hit the jackpot!" it baldly said.

It was no doubt well-meant but I viewed it as extremely damaging. I could well imagine Vien pointing it out to the Committee, saying "Look at this proof: the Canadian is just another mercenary." This hurt deeply; it mattered to me that I was viewed as a reporter who nobody owned.

I could imagine the Foreign Ministry committee listening to Vien with some sympathy before weighing its priorities. But though that cable hurt, the vodka helped.

It meant another night on the plank, but now we were a happy band, ready for anything, we thought, not yet knowing, not yet emotionally drained by what lay ahead. The knowledge that our film was wanted, perhaps worldwide, was a much-needed rush. It gave me hope that my eventual documentary would find an audience beyond the norm — one that would ask questions and demand answers, though I knew well enough that on television, however emotional the story, the next tragedy would quickly overtake it.

I knew the correspondent in the field can seldom ever change how the Big Story ends, and that was the frustration, the futility that came to colour the job. The need was to see further than the moment, a need to go back in time and see the news as history revisited, a need to share, preserve, and document the memories of others, so that with that evidence judgment became easier for later generations.

That last evening at our hideout beyond Phu Ly, the town reduced to a tombstone, I began to type detailed notes on what I'd seen and heard so far, driven by the need that over the years, however long the time, I could tell myself *I* did not forget.

If Phu Ly was an example of what was to come on our journey — a retracing of places now existing only on old maps — then I felt it a special responsibility to record whatever possible, to carefully attribute what was stated as fact, to point to exaggeration and bias, but then to judge it all as best I could. It was early days and my first impression that the North Vietnamese were fighting largely in the name of nationalism, not Marxism, needed a great deal more verification.

But certainly it was here in the North that the Vietnam War would be determined. It was crucial that I remain constantly aware of the historical nature of our filming. I was seeing what no other foreign journalist had seen, but while the camera could convey much of the evidence, it could not interpret and evaluate what it recorded.

There are times when the journalistic creed of objectivity is merely a cover for ignorance, or worse a pandering to politics and patriotism, a betrayal of the truth. Setting out the next day down Highway 1, along the flight path of the bombers, I vowed to miss nothing.

Alas, good intentions felt washed away as we began our onward journey, the rains hitting us in what seemed aerial tidal waves. Yet these were merely fringe showers spilling over from the September monsoon, rendering this section of the westward mountains a hell on Earth for the armies on the Ho Chi Minh Trail.

Our drive had slowed to a crawl, two bobbing jeeps inching forward with their occupants maintaining grim silence. Vu in the front seat had a sheltering roll-up window, but at the back, where Fujii and I were wedged, the jeep had canvas flaps in place of windows, and every so often, with startling suddenness, the flaps blew in another thrashing of leaden rain. Fujii never complained but about once a minute an horrendous sigh like some mournful clarinet would burst from his lungs, a sound so repetitive that Vu couldn't help laughing, while I attempted to escape from it all by bending my head to my knees.

I now relied on Vu to alert me as to how far we'd come and to any sign of life that we could try to film should the rain recede. After several hours, when Vu suddenly shouted "Thanh Hoa, Mike-san," I quickly looked ahead, expecting busy streets and people everywhere. But as we drew nearer it was apparent that although a large town, Thanh Hoa was now a total ruin and uninhabitable.

Again, going by the jeep's odometer, we were precisely at the point where pre-war maps placed Thanh Hoa. And unlike Phu Ly, some recognizable evidence remained. Here and there, I could see a brick wall still partly standing. Elsewhere, in a scene like a stage setting of life and death, a huge high archway, once the entry to some grand building, now stood all alone, oddly intact. Through the arch I could see distant palm trees bowing to the rubble.

Beneath the great arch, on the former main street, a vendor tended a cartload of bottled water, fruit, and rice cakes as if nothing had happened. We were just eighty miles from Hanoi in the provincial capital of the most populous of the southern provinces, home to two million people until the bombing began. No one lived here anymore; nowhere could I see any rebuilding despite the year-long bombing halt.

Yet there was a constant flow of people, old men straining behind their "iron horses" laden with fifty-kilogram rice bags, older women balancing immense weights of cloth and cooked food on the bicycles they pushed. Gradually, as we filmed, a pattern emerged. Sometimes these human mules would arrive one by one, sometimes by the dozen, as if clocking in to work, then they would all pause for a time at the vendor's cart at the landmark archway. From long routine, from all over the province, they met here to freshen up, then team up for the long, hard haul westward toward the "Trail" or East to the coast. In effect, Thanh Hoa remained what it had always been: the main distribution centre on the route south. We were witness to how fundamentally the bombing had failed.

Yet on another level, LBJ and the U.S. military had achieved total success. For year after year the Pentagon had misled the American public and the American media into believing that Rolling Thunder was largely limited to the air war over the "Trail," where the bombing still continued, or strictly to military targets on the North itself. Yet North Vietnam perforce had shared in the deceit. At Thanh Hoa, so close to Hanoi, I kept asking myself, how could such devastation not become known? How possibly could one nation bomb another all-out every day for four years and the outside world know nothing about it?

Yet that was the case. My Japanese colleagues had never previously travelled south from Hanoi, and from their shocked expression, and from the disbelief shown by our minders at the wholesale destruction, it was clear all this was widely unknown within the North. Even those who had lived in the southern provinces for the most part knew only their own local plight; a strict system of separate regional co-operatives meant there was little communication and even less travel between provinces. At this time, the North had no television, only state-controlled radio, and foreigners, whether living in or visiting Hanoi, were not allowed to travel south on the explanation that it was too dangerous, as indeed it was.

For Hanoi, any admission of the massive destruction while the bombing continued, and when it could be renewed at any time, might seriously risk endangering national morale, even though the secrecy year after year encouraged ever more random bombing! But then why had Hanoi approved our filming? Seemingly because with the formal Paris peace talks and the parallel Kissinger secret negotiations hopelessly stalled, public opinion mattered as never before.

Apparently, Hanoi felt it time to reach out to an increasingly anti-war American public and perhaps felt that allowing in a neutral journalist from America's closest neighbour was the way to do it.

I had been closely watching the activity at the Thanh Hoa archway for two hours or so before the pattern became clearer. Though each new arrival made his or her way to the vendor's cart for water and food, there was never any money exchanged. Nor did any of them linger. The vendor, I learned, was a senior cadre giving instructions. For the women he pointed his arm east or north where dirt tracks led to the hideouts of the young, nomadic female "shock brigades," while for the men the direction was always toward the Western "Trail."

On the "iron horses" the women pushed I saw mostly bundled clothing and toiletry, on those of the men bales of rice, vegetables, and medicines strapped to metal rods welded between handlebars and saddles. Once loaded, they set off in small groups, symbolically pushing forward.

Leaving the ruined market town which had been the pride of the French during their eighty-year occupation, a town wasted in as many seconds, we too headed west, soon passing first one then another of the primitive bicycle convoys. It was impossible not to be moved — and disturbed — by the sight: the old men looking misshapen, heads bent almost to the handlebars, lives sacrificed this way all through their mid-fifties to mid-sixties, if they lasted that long, now jogging at a reckless pace given their 200-kilogram burdens. Every so often a lone cyclist would rush alongside to hand out bottled water which the old men would sip as they ran, at times in the 100-degree-plus heat emptying the bottles over their heads.

Seeing it, the sheer grit and determination, I thought of the Tour de France, but this was much harder — and much nobler.

Speeding by them in our jeep, I think we all felt a vague unease, as if somehow we should help, yet our own dirt-ride soon proved the roughest so far. Again, every few feet, or wherever the rain failed to drain at the roadside, the subsequent sun had baked neat mounds of mud, looking just like road-stops but so numerous and stretching for so many miles that in the jeep body and nerves felt entirely shattered. When the torment ceased it was thanks to groups of boys nearing their teens who at every quarter mile were smoothing the road, just as they had on the way to Nam Dinh. Clearly, this rural use of older boys freed the mobilized young women to stay nearer their priority, Highway 1. We were now far from it, in terrain that led to the Truong Son range.

It was like coming out of the wilderness into a kind of forested national park. And, arriving for much needed siesta, climbing a short way, up a rock path beneath high cedars, the "guest house" this time had us all surprised: actual beds, four of them for the crew, Vu, and myself. Each had a bedside table and drawers and a kerosene lamp. It was so surprising and comforting that it took a moment to realize we were in a cave!

CHAPTER SEVEN
The Cave People

AWAKE AND OUTSIDE THE cave, falling rain from the cliff above became our shower, a bucket dug deep our toilet. In the distance, we could hear various voices, even laughter, and from the hillside strange mechanical sounds.

Puzzled, we sat waiting at the entrance of our cave until our designated host arrived. He had brought a flask of green tea, handing us paper cups, then introducing himself: Dr. Thien Dien in perfect, no-nonsense English he said, "What can I tell you?"

"Where are we?" I said, and we laughed.

"Welcome to Cam Binh, our nation's newest village. And its best! It's about a half mile from here. Shall we go?"

Refreshed, keen, curious, I sensed this shoot would be very different. As we walked, Dr. Dien explained he was a pediatrician and therefore was "Needed here to help civilians rather than" — and he gestured to the far off mountains — "there with our troops." He had been trained in London during the mid-fifties after the North gained independence and I guessed he was not just a doctor but a senior Party man. He had managed a major hospital at Ky Anh until that district was wiped out, then got the task of helping create a new model village, Cam Binh, meaning "Precious Peace." As if biblically, it had been created in just seven days the previous October, 1968, soon after the bombing pause, with the objective of rebuilding rural life "with the safety of the caves nearby."

"Here we are. Go wherever you like. Time for questions later." And with that he left us on a hillside looking down on terraced rice fields glinting jade-green in the late afternoon sun.

This was our first sight in the southern provinces of near-normal human existence: homes, stores, offices, schools, all with mud walls and straw roofs but a functioning community, even though just a one-of-a-kind "experiment."

I would learn that 3,200 people in thirty spaced-out hamlets had relocated here and were given exceptional autonomy. The ruling Politburo had long since learned that its early rigid control of agriculture endangered the primary goal of a unified Vietnam. Now, the older women tending the rice paddies as we filmed, rifles over their right shoulders, huge smiles under conical hats, were basically the rulers of all they surveyed. Food prices were still controlled by the state, but farmers here now received 5 percent of everything they sold, with no limit on volume. It was a lenient, if convenient approach to rehabilitating the millions of evacuees in the southern provinces, essential to a long-haul war.

We stayed two days at Cam Binh, contented cavemen because we could film without hindrance the reality of the North at war. We slept well and ate well without the exhausting back and forth to Highway 1 which we must soon face again. Like the villagers (but wholly unlike the life of a foreign correspondent), I now thrived on routine: the bell that rang late morning as classes finished for the day, the sight of children teaming up for their beloved volleyball and football, carefree despite being born to war and despite the obligatory and indoctrinating red neckbands of Communist Youth which they all wore at all times.

Leaving the playground, we saw an urgent maternity case being carried on a stretcher to another straw-roofed hut, but one that seemed far too small and primitive to be a clinic.

We followed them inside, amazed to find a sloped walkway extending deep below ground and there a makeshift medical ward with a dozen beds, anaesthetic drips, and an operating sector. It had suction pumps to handle any flooding and a separate emergency entry/exit.

Here we watched as a midwife took over, a tradition encouraged because unlike in China, the Vietnamese could choose when they'd marry and the number of children they wanted. This meant that midwives largely replaced the doctors needed in the evacuated hospitals, hidden from the bombers in caves high on the mountain slopes. The nearest such hospital was ruled forbidden for filming, but I learned that it served ninety thousand evacuees with beds for just ninety, a one in a thousand chance of admission. So relocating and recreating rural life, and encouraging rural autonomy and self-sufficiency on family matters was key to victory. With some four million pre-teen children, including a great many war orphans to care for, Cam Binh was a blueprint for the renewal of ancient village values and traditions — ironically, essentially the opposite of what was occurring in South Vietnam, where village life was a free-fire zone oppressed by *both* sides.

As we left the underground clinic, air raid sirens echoed everywhere, startling us, but it was a twice-weekly "readiness" rehearsal.

In the paddy fields, AA guns shed their camouflage as women militia scanned the skies. The playground children now formed pre-arranged lines, gradually joined by teachers and any family members in the village. Then, in multi-formation, they headed for the hills and the specific caves allotted them, there to take siesta and after, in family groups, to cleanse their cave and attend to its camouflage before returning to their new village homes.

We stayed on, keen to film the workplace caves, difficult filming because of the dim battery light and sparse air supply, the heat intensified by the constant whirling metal of vehicle repairs, or the chattering new textile looms from China, or the screeching drills widening the sides of the caves to create more production space. For secrecy, the cave factories had no names, just triple-digit numbers coded for the type of production. Each evacuated industry had been divided and allocated to different caves as a safeguard against the "smart" guided bombs the U.S. was known to be developing, and against the ever-existing perils of nature, not least the frequent drip-drip from the dark, jagged rock above their heads which at times became a sudden deluge, forcing evacuation once again.

Gratefully leaving the dank factory caves for the now-cool sun, we returned to the rice fields in time for the evening irrigation — a foot-pedal method as ancient as Vietnam itself. It captured the still-primitive nature of the north and, paradoxically, its assured survival. What the years of saturation bombing didn't and couldn't do was cripple a largely straw-hut agricultural society which could rebuild, like Cam Binh, faster than the bombers could fly.

From what we had seen so far in the southern provinces, every aspect of modern civilization the French had built or established in their eighty-year occupation had been erased by their ally in this proxy Cold War.

But though nothing of brick and mortar remained intact, the traditional rural village, wherever possible, still thrived.

Early evening we found the children back from their emergency cave homes and back at school together with grandparents, the children helping their elders to learn to read and write. It had been quite an education, Cam Binh, not least for us! We shared a final meal with Dr. Dien, noting down his answers to a hundred and one questions. We were all very pleased — such great footage! Then we were all somewhat down. One last night as cavemen and then again the unknown of Highway 1. Suddenly I felt apprehensive.

After Cam Binh, the journey south seemed ever more surreal and dismaying. Our jeeps were the only vehicles to be seen, except for the very occasional military truck. Mile after mile we saw no human life, nor evidence of it other than the now-sparse nomadic bands of young women tending the highway, for the degree of destruction heightened the further we went. Waterlogged bomb craters were everywhere, as random and numerous as the mosquitos breeding in them. By the roadside, piles of dumped debris awaited the distant day when garbage trucks might safely remove it all: contorted bicycles, twisted window frames, splintered school desks, shredded clothing torn from the dead. The unending sight of so much sorrow silenced us, and reaching our immediate destination, Vinh, the scene was no different. It too was dead.

Vinh had been the newest town in the entire republic, built in 1955 soon after the Geneva Conventions, whose majority membership pledged national elections within two years. A small coastal fishing town, it once had a rail line but now, like Phu Ly, only bits of twisted metal here and there spoke of its brief existence.

We didn't stay, pressing on to town of Ha Thinh, which had been a rice and agricultural trading centre of just twelve thousand people, and though now totally deserted, in a macabre way parts of buildings still stood, like upright skeletons.

The unrelenting bombing had begun August 5, 1965, said Nguyen Huy Thinh, the cadre who met us, and he claimed there were 2,200 air attacks on this one town alone in the last month before the "pause." Ha Thinh was the last town nearest to the 17th Parallel and had been an easy target for U.S. fighter-bombers based on aircraft carriers minutes away in international waters.

Just outside the town I saw the remnants of a secondary school where Thinh said 750 students had been in class when navy bombers first struck in '65, and four years later torn books and school papers and crumpled desks still littered the ruins. Isolated a mile from town, the municipal hospital, bombed seventeen times Thinh said, was now such a heap of rubble that all that could be seen was part of a Red Cross sign that had presumably been clearly visible on the hospital roof.

We were packing to leave when, surprisingly, a jeep pulled up beside us, the one passenger introducing himself as Pham Van Bach, Chief Justice of the Supreme Court of the Democratic Republic of Vietnam. He too was documenting the consequences of the four years of all-out bombing, which he insisted was little realized even in high circles in Hanoi. He was very emotional, and in a filmed interview, when asked about the hundreds of captive American pilots, he said "I call them air pirates. They are war criminals subject to the jurisdiction of the DRV courts. In my view they should have been punished, but the government still gives them humane treatment."

Was he hinting at what might occur should the peace talks fail?

Coming from the Chief Justice, his remarks were troubling, though very likely he had little influence with the DRV leadership. Even so, somehow I needed to approach Prime Minister Pham Van Dong on the POW issue — the major concern of the American public.

For our crew, and myself in particular, a far more immediate drama lay ahead. We had planned one more film location for the day, at Dong Hoi, the closest village to the 17th Parallel and the DMZ, the partitioned demilitarized zone.

But I would never discover the fate of Dong Hoi, for abruptly Highway 1 came to end. Where the road must have risen between small hills there were now layers of interlocking bomb craters, so many they were impassable other than at the considerable risk of skirting them on foot.

From where our jeeps had halted, where Highway 1 ended, the full perspective of this cratered world was lost. I looked hesitantly at Fujii, but he nodded knowingly, and because filming here might take hours it was agreed that Lam and Ishigaki, in the second jeep, would head a few miles back and then find a route westward in search of some haven for the night. Then Fujii with just his camera, leaving the heavy tripod behind, very cautiously led the way between craters until some twenty minutes later the two of us reached the maximum hill height. For minutes we just stared all around in disbelief.

East to west, literally thousands of massive bomb craters reshaped the horizon. The very hills had been bombed, shredded, to render them impassable.

As the camera rolled, I tried to imagine describing it if I had not personally seen it, and I began. "If some extraterrestrial being was to land here, what planet would he believe he was on? Not even the Moon is cratered like this." Hyperbole? Not if you were there! Starting at the region of Dong Hoi — doubtless once a short route for troops trekking in the night to the Ho Chi Minh Trail — the sliver of land that is Vietnam narrows, curving inward, reduced to just a few miles between the mountains and the coast. But now, high enough that we actually stood on grass, the entire view west or east or south toward the DMZ was of endless adjoining craters, the work of countless days of B-52 "carpet" bombing.

We filmed in every direction! Then, from our perch on a safe patch of grass, we puzzled how we'd get back down to the distant jeep, how to circle this vast necklace of craters. Climbing up, we could wedge into the earth with the tip of our boots, but descending on our heels meant certain disaster. Fujii's solution was to slowly slide down on our butts!

Even so, there was little solid space between the myriad craters. The smallest were fifteen to thirty feet across, the largest interlocking with others to become mini-canals filled, and constantly refilled, by the monsoon rains — and mosquitos.

Here, countless squadrons of B-52s had flown six hours from Guam or the Philippines day after day, year after year, to render this particular width of Vietnam wholly uninhabitable, assuming the carnage extended beyond our view, as it must have. This was journey's end. We would never get to Vinh Linh, the border "city" where we'd been told seventy thousand guerrillas, many of them families, lived deep underground, patrolling the border zone at night and at all times accepting extreme deprivation and imminent death.

And here we were sticking our own necks out a bit too far!

"We go," I said to Fujii, and after snapping photos with the small Nikon he kept in a waterproof waist-pouch, we began the slippery descent.

Even sliding down we couldn't help going faster than we should have. Fujii went ahead and "made land," and I thought I would, but coupled with the debilitating heat, the intense headache and muscle ache that had beset me during the past day or so suddenly, violently returned just as I tried to slide through a space between two craters hardly wider than my skinny frame. In this numbed state I felt a certainty that the deep water crater to my left had my number! Fear like none I had ever known sharpened my pounding headache into a hammer blow — and mercifully I blacked out.

I awoke in my room at the Thong Nhat Hotel with Vu and Fujii there.

"Dengue, we think," Fujii said.

I knew of dengue fever as a mosquito-transmitted type of flu which for a short time attacked the muscles, causing extreme fatigue. There was no vaccine or specific medication for dengue fever. Faced with sickness and sudden danger, my brain had abruptly shut down. But while lasting several days, the fever and hallucinating could just as suddenly end, and precautions had been taken. Unknown to me, our jeep driver, with heavy ropes to clutch, had been climbing towards us as we descended between the great necklace of craters and he had reached me at the ultimate, crucial second. But perhaps because they were charged with my well-being, Vu and Fugii-san were vague on further details. For three days they had been feeding me chicken broth and green tea. Now I felt just fine, almost as if nothing untoward had happened. I got up, dressed, and hugged each of them. It had been tough on them, too.

Back at Dong Loc, after I had fainted, our jeep was joined by that of Lam, who had not yet found any rest place. It was decided that my condition was too uncertain to risk any lengthy side trips in search of rest and food. The lead jeep would drive nonstop to Hanoi without food or siesta, and the second jeep would follow slowly. They had placed me on the back seat, Vu and Fujii taking turns holding me up to keep me from falling over, and had sped through the dark for four hundred kilometres in a record forty hours!

"Mr. Tran is coming to see you," Vu said, and as if on cue Tran arrived, bringing a batch of cables. I scanned them. The Network wanted an hour documentary ASAP. This time NBC would excerpt it over several days on their main evening newscast. As I read this aloud, Vu said there was an ICC flight leaving that night for Vientiane, connecting to Hong Kong–Toronto, and reading the next cable, I was anxious to be on that flight. What I read was the best news I'd ever heard: "Baby arriving late March — love Mariko."

We all hugged again and now Tran (having of course read all cables!) produced a bottle of vodka to toast what the North had never known, as Tran put it, "A child to be born to peace." It was the most beautiful sentiment.

I had been away in North Vietnam almost six weeks and, except for my arrival cable, Mariko had heard nothing from me. There was still no means of phoning, and there was still the documentary to produce. I could only cable her that I should be home in two weeks or so. And right then, with all of us laughing, I got my suitcase and started packing.

As Tran left, I walked with him to the lobby, wondering how to phrase what I needed to say. Casually, I told him that at Ha Thinh I had met the Chief Justice and heard his views on the POW issue. Tran nodded as if familiar with this.

I told him, "I'm sure you know that among the American public the condition of the POWs is just about the most important factor in any peace settlement — and while I am hugely pleased with our filming, it does not address that vital factor —"

Tran interjected, "What are you trying to say?"

"I would like to return if granted filming access to the POW camps."

"For a reporter that would be a first, wouldn't it?" he said somewhat bitingly.

"It might be a breakthrough — much needed," I retorted.

Tran changed the subject. "By the way, did you know you had an unlikely first? Our Soviet friends, after attending the president's funeral, lingered too long in Peking, so Moscow television used your report. Only the Kremlin could have decided that."

"Really? I hope the Kremlin censor left it alone."

Tran laughed. "You ask for too much."

Women at war are thanked by General Giap, the victor of Dien Bien Phu in 1954.

Female soldiers are greeted by General Van Tien Dung upon victory in 1975.

The bomb-cratered infinity near the DMZ. (Photo by Ryoko Fujii.)

The children of Nam Dinh, a city devastated by B-52 bombing.

Civilian women travelled anywhere and everywhere to clear bomb damage.

A million women and young people lived a nomadic life mending roads and clearing craters.

Young female militia on guard while their elders ploughed the fields.

Surviving landmarks of bombed towns became strategic meeting places.

The straw-hut guest house near the slopes of the Ho Chi Minh Trail.

The author's wood-plank bed.

A typical cave factory for evacuated industries.

Militia clear a bomb crater on Highway 1 during the bombing years,
1965–68.

CHAPTER EIGHT
The Kremlin People

OUR OWN KREMLIN IN Toronto, as all minions of the Network well knew, was a Victorian mansion for senior management. It stood alone and aloof, a large Jarvis Street compound, with the production warrens of radio and television out of sight — and, it often seemed, out of mind. Here, the many bosses of bosses ruled with an iron whim, seldom seen but much heard. How the Kremlin label arose is lost to obscurity, but the name fitted the Network's cult of management, which could do no wrong even as it did it.

Just back from Hanoi, I went first to the newsroom to report to foreign affairs manager Ron Robbins. A fellow immigrant, he was much respected for his journalistic credentials, though a stern man. In his office you stood unless invited to sit — and this time I was not. There was no "well done," just a perfunctory "welcome back" and then an astonishing "Michael, RCMP Ottawa wants to talk to you about your travels in North Vietnam." I wondered what interest the RCMP could have other than perhaps acting for the Pentagon.

I kept silent and was then told, "We think you should go." But I noticed he said "we," not "I."

"Robbie, anything I have to say will be in the documentary."

He slowly nodded, as if he too found the whole matter distasteful. "Ah, the documentary. We've scheduled it a week from now, a full hour on *Thursday Night*."

That meant just seven days to edit, script, narrate, and mix.

"That's near impossible, Robbie."

But he knew I wasn't arguing. "And Knowlton wants a rough cut two days before." So the seven days now became five days.

That was it — soldier dismissed! I felt too rattled to linger in the newsroom. As a condition of getting our colour film out uncensored, I had agreed to respect military information Hanoi deemed classified.

Now I felt that journalistic ethics were being betrayed. Dammit, we were reporters, not spies. In a depressed mood, I made my way past the Kremlin to the motel opposite — the first Four Seasons — where the foreign correspondents always stayed. At the bar, Bacardi and Coke in hand, I was no less concerned that Knowlton Nash, a long-time friend and now a Kremlin occupant, seemed in no hurry to see me. I sensed a coolness from senior management but thought it unlikely that Knowlton had suggested the proposed RCMP debriefing, for he'd know I would decline. More likely, after my first reports from Hanoi, widely shown on U.S. networks, the Pentagon was exerting pressure wherever it could and the Network management, even when in part disagreement, would concede to whomever in their ranks felt the most righteous on any issue. Oh well, no time to dwell on it!

By the second Bacardi, even the five-day time challenge seemed for the best — hopefully it would speed my return home. On arrival in Toronto, I had called Mariko. Had anyone from the London bureau enquired about her well-being? No one from Management had called her, but our London-based camera crews, Ed Higginson and his wife Pat, and Phil and his then wife Barbara Pendry, had been extra kind. We talked about baby names for a boy or girl, and I promised to take extended leave nearing the birth. Mariko's calmness helped immensely. Five days to deliver an historical first — now I felt it could be done!

It was a comfort, too, working with Bill Harcourt, perhaps the most likeable program executive in the entire network. His style was to ensure you got what you needed while staying out until the final cut. I asked for two editors round the clock and got two of the best: Ronald Garrant and George Domnas.

For speed, we decided against the sophisticated, safer but slower tablefixed Steenbeck in favour of a real oldie: a foot-pedal device that powered the footage through a small eye-level screen. Intended for fast, short productions, it meant snapping off preferred scenes, then hanging the selected film "takes" on inch-long nails protruding from a five-foot-wide wooden bin, cloth-lined to prevent scratching of the film. Technically, it was as primitive as could be and we all had a good laugh when finding the scene of ancient pedal-irrigation in the Vietnam rice-fields. But this old method of selecting then splicing to an assembly reel enabled rapid editing, and this way I could script and/or amend sequences as the editors completed them.

The documentary I now had just five days to prepare would be the most important of my career and would be the first-ever footage seen by Americans of North Vietnam at war — this after fifteen years of U.S. involvement in Vietnam and after five years of bitter combat. The doc had to be beyond reproach. I had to make crystal clear the difference between what I had personally seen and what I had merely been told, and make clear that I had accepted filming restrictions on military-related scenes in return for bringing out our colour footage totally uncensored.

I blocked out four fifteen-minute major sequences, two for each editor. (1) We'd open the film with Ho Chi Minh's 1945 Declaration of Independence, its beginning word for word that of the United States. Then the journey through the cratered land wrought by four years of non-stop bombing. (2) We'd show how the people of the North had coped physically and mentally, especially the role of women. (3) We'd show Hanoi's dependence on ancient Vietnamese traditions and the nationalism that accommodated Marxism. (4) Finally, a fuller account of the death of Ho Chi Minh and the even greater defiance this had brought.

We worked sixteen-hour days, with the two editors smiling; they were making a killing, deservedly, on overtime. In contrast, the foreign correspondents, when necessary — which was often — worked round the clock for no extra pay.

(Some forty-five years later, reviewing my film archives with Brock Silversides, head of Media Commons at Robarts Library, University of Toronto, I'm refreshing my memory and checking the hard facts for this narrative: the "evidence" — scripts and transcripts, the notes typed daily during that first filming of North Vietnam, the press and public reaction (both Canadian and American) to our films, the gradually ever more

angry exchange of cables and letters between myself and Management —
and, like a bad joke long forgotten, the Network contracts for its foreign
correspondents. These were only for one year at a time, no matter how
long you'd been in the field, the clear intent being to breed insecurity and
robotic obedience.

In the early sixties, or ten years into Canadian television, there was
no war zone insurance, no health coverage. From my post as Far East
Correspondent, based in Tokyo, the numerous assignments to South
Vietnam were at my own risk. On one occasion, fortunately flying back
from Saigon to Toronto for year-end meetings, I was rushed to the
Doctor's Hospital with severe hepatitis, the cause countless leech bites
that clung to my legs as I waded in a stream with an ARVN patrol preparing to attack a suspected Viet Cong hideout. For six weeks I was in
intensive care, with the hospital bill of $1,200 being far more than my
meagre savings. The Network paid the bill but then deducted it from my
salary — $100 every month for a year! Even by the mid-to-late sixties, as
London Correspondent, the base salary of $13,400 a year came with the
Dickensian condition "Your services shall be available … every day of
the month including statutory and religious holidays."

There was no overtime for foreign correspondents, no matter the cir-
cumstance. The year I got into North Vietnam — target of the heaviest
bombing in the history of war — the Network agreed to "hardship pay"
for correspondents in war zones. The amount was $50 a week! I never
claimed it — I didn't want to feel so worthless.

Re-reading the contract so many decades later, it captured, I felt, the
profile and failure of TV's senior program management, almost entirely
old hands from radio with little understanding of the medium of television
with its vastly different needs and pressures. Thus for decades the Network
became a paradox of an unchanging management and an ever evolving,
creative workforce which — to my mind — alone justified the state network's existence. As a result, through the fifties, sixties, into the seventies,
morale was abysmal, with a seemingly ceaseless management–union war
of filed reprimands and grievances.

Yet despite it all I loved the job — I think we all did, and if needs be I
would somehow have paid them for it! For me, for so long, the Network —
despite its management — reflected Canada, and so there was a sense of

nation building. In that context, revisiting those years through my archives, I realized the Network would always be a part of me.)

Editing on the old contraption brought back memories of how I joined the Network: as a rewrite man for the nightly TV news. That was 1955, and I was twenty-five, though I had been a cub reporter on Fleet Street for many years. Apart from the oddity of having to swear allegiance to the queen (never required in Britain), the Network epitomized the New World: new country, new medium, new opportunity.

I was lucky — I got the job nobody else wanted! Film clips from international agencies like Visnews were beginning to pour in, but these at first clashed with the newsroom style, then "rip and read," news literally torn from the wire feeds of Canadian Press or AP or Reuters with no visual images. For a great many years the Network saw its obligation as simple news-relay rather than costly — and controversial — news-gathering. The coming of news-film clips with their scenes of war and want were deemed somewhat indecent and for sure a passing fad, rather like colour television, which news management resisted until the mid-sixties ("Why do we need it?" the news chief asked a group of us, and someone bellowed "Because blood is red!"). Not least, film clips meant extra, painstaking work — screening them, cutting them to size, rewriting the wire copy to fit the visuals. So, like some despised lower caste, an editor and I were housed well out of sight in a rented room across the street!

At first it was a challenge, a puzzle, writing to film so that the right words matched the right images. But I figured out a system of how many letters, or spaces, would equal any given length of 16mm film — three feet being five seconds, five feet equalling eight seconds, and so on. It enabled exact, quick editing. Film required its own script style; the eye could absorb far more than the ear, so literal description had to be avoided. So too all the usual trite adjectives now unneeded because they flashed through the viewer's mind as he or she watched, like as not changing ideas and feelings about the wider world. Television news was becoming humanity's first emotionally participatory medium!

Soon the agency film clips were much longer, with information more complex than the seventeen-minute nightly newscast could handle. In late

1955, the Network decided that the existing Sunday night *Newsmagazine*, a half-hour of oddities, should have a live, topical version. Perhaps by default, "the film guy" got the job of editor (Management then preferred newspaper titles; the senior TV title of producer was many years away, at least at the network news). With another newcomer, Morley Safer, as deputy editor and co-writer, the format was three updated issues of the week, each film about ten minutes in length. But as much as possible the film had to be original footage, so we hired two cameramen, Phil Pendry and Bob Crone, who'd go anywhere, any hellhole, for $35 a day. Instead of staff announcers, as host we brought in acclaimed National Film Board director Gordon Burwash, and to stay immediate we scripted right up to airtime.

With Morley I found a shared fascination with the power of news film to arouse public opinion and concern. And the program's timing was just right (with the very early Network management encouraging initiative). For Canadian television, 1956 onward was the first era of great global events, the Hungarian revolution, the Anglo-French invasion of Egypt and seizure of the Suez Canal, and the emergence of Canada's Lester Pearson as global peacemaker.

Soon *Newsmagazine* was must-watch, but more than that, to a considerable degree it hastened the development of a skilled television core of foreign correspondents, bringing a Canadian view of the wider world. Even so, overall the Network kept to its preference that only staff announcers should narrate news reportage, and for Morley and I, both in our mid-twenties, the growing ambition to become foreign correspondents ourselves was then just laughable. Neither of us could have imagined that in that role, before very long, both of us would be tested in a war not then even in the news: 'Nam.

We finished the North Vietnam documentary, titled *Ho Chi Minh's People*, in four days and sent a copy, written and narrated, to the Network's Kremlin for comment, but for two days heard nothing back. I didn't see it on air. I had been pre-booked to hand-deliver a copy of the documentary to NBC in New York and, if asked, to assist with excerpts for their main evening newscast.

I was about to leave the motel for the airport when I was hailed by a familiar voice who said, "Great doc — saw it yesterday."

"Seriously? I didn't hear of any screening."

A long-time friend, he hesitated before saying, "Maybe because there were two unknowns at the screening."

"What do you mean — from the networks?"

"No, but for sure Americans, maybe Pentagon, maybe Embassy." I was stunned. Could I believe him? Yes, he was in a position to know.

"How come you were there?" I asked, and he explained that if the film hadn't been ready for *Thursday Night* it was to be run over two nights on the news section of *Weekend*, the new Saturday-Sunday hour.

"Who told you, who else was there?" But my friend just rolled his eyes as if to say he'd already said too much. "Well, how did it end?"

"For me, I was crying at the end at the Ho funeral scenes," he said. "As for the two Americans, at the end they just walked out, one of them saying 'Pinko crap.'"

Certainly, no RCMP would talk like that, so the shocking conclusion was that the Network, conveniently ignoring me, had shown the film to a foreign power before it would be seen by the Canadian public. All the way to New York I felt a sickening betrayal.

I dared not mention this to NBC, or they would most likely not run the film, and I couldn't challenge the Kremlin for an explanation because they would realize who my source was. So once again in dealings with Management I had to bury my disgust.

In the field, the correspondent expected and accepted uncertainty while relying on Management to be totally trustworthy. But again and again it was anything but. Most recently, in mid-1968, I had been abruptly ordered back from my past as London correspondent for three months of "rehabilitation." Management gave no specific reason, nor had any idea what I was to do, finally suggesting I take a course at Ryerson in television studio directing, totally irrelevant to news reporting — this in a year when news events were ever more startling. Later, a friend in senior management confided that constant complaints from the British High Commissioner in Ottawa on my London reportage motivated my recall.

Then, by happenstance, Knowlton Nash rescued me. While in Toronto, he and Romeo LeBlanc, London correspondent for Radio-Canada and a man I knew to be kind and thoughtful, approached me to ask if I'd take over Knowlton's role as president of the Foreign Correspondents Association. I agreed, surprised soon after when Romeo became Prime Minister Trudeau's press secretary, and Knowlton, previously Washington correspondent, joined Management at the Kremlin as head of News and Current Affairs — the first such role with implications of a major reshaping of both management and programming. The foreign correspondents cheered Knowlton's move. One of us, daylight at last, we thought.

Immediately, after Knowlton's move to Management, I called to ask him why I was idling in Toronto while the "Prague Spring" challenged the communist world. He quickly responded, "Get there ASAP, if at all possible." I had just one day in London, telling Mariko, who had been with me on several European and Mideast assignments, that this one was too dicey. Within a few hours with cameraman Phil Pendry I was driving up and down the Austrian-Czech border searching for a police post that would let us through.

We had the camera gear hidden in the spare tire, Phil saying that he was a botanist, me an archaeologist, and while we might have looked the part we didn't fool the sympathetic border guard who finally waved us on without any search. We arrived in Prague at the same time as the first Soviet tanks, which began firing at random.

After twelve hours filming the carnage and Czech defiance we hastened back to Vienna, and to an equally big story. Czechs were streaming into Austria by the thousands, a great many besieging the Canadian Embassy for refugee status.

I told Phil to film it all and I'd be back in a couple of days, then, clutching our Prague footage and leaving my baggage with Phil, I got an Air Canada flight to Toronto. With the time difference in my favour, I wrote the script and edit instructions during the flight and the result was an eleven-minute eyewitness report leading the nightly newscast well before the U.S. networks began satellite feeds from Vienna. I had not slept for forty-eight hours, but felt pleased.

Late the next morning, August 28, 1968, I was ordered to report to the manager of Radio News and there was reprimanded for "leaving your post" without permission. Then it was television's turn. I was reprimanded a second time by the senior news manager who read out a quite bitter complaint from the vice-president of Radio-Canada, furious that I had refused to hand over my cameraman and his gear to their correspondent, who'd gotten into Prague but without any equipment.

I explained the big story developing in Vienna and my plan to return there and to Prague, whereupon — the reprimand completed — I was ordered to get there immediately! Once more, Management had played its demoralizing habit of allowing any single disgruntled member to vent anger without any consensus — and without even a word of recognition of what had just been achieved.

Some two weeks later, after a third documentary aired in prime time, a letter to me from Knowlton seemed like a promise of change:

Dear Mike,

In all your travelling about you might not have noticed that President George Davidson spoke very highly of your Czechoslovakian programs in a recent speech in Ottawa. He said: 'How many of you have followed in recent weeks the unfolding Czechoslovakian crisis and tragedy through the eyes and voice of Michael Maclear? I have seen three half-hour programs over the CBC on this subject, each one of superb quality, revealing in its depths of perception, sensitivity and insight, as the tragedy of the Czech people in the grip of their valiant struggle to achieve freedom unfolded before our very eyes.

'How much was this worth to the Canadian television viewer? This was no second-hand pickup of another net-work production. This was Canadian production, this was CBC production, and I firmly believe that there were numbers of Canadians viewing these programs who said to themselves these programs alone are worth the cost to us of maintaining our public broadcasting institution in Canada.'

But there was no retraction of the earlier reprimands from Management, and technically I was still on recall for "rehabilitation."

It took another letter from the president — this one to the network board of directors quoting U.S. Embassy kudos for my Prague coverage — to get me restored to my London correspondent roll, perhaps because the U.S. Embassy far outranked the British High Commission in influence. But soon after I was recalled to Toronto, this time instead of being cast into limbo I was asked to help shape Knowlton's dream project, what eventually became *Weekend*.

I had agreed out of respect for Knowlton and what I felt were our shared ideas for advancing factual programming. The concept was a first-ever News and Current Affairs co-production — a symbolic step toward merging the two divisions, or at least reducing their idiotic rivalry and costly duplication of management, which bred waste and indifference. While producing *Newsmagazine*, we'd often call a prospective interviewee only to be told "But your Current Affairs crew is here now." Neither division ever exchanged notes of intended shoots. At times the distrust was bizarre.

In the late fifties, as the Network's roving correspondent for News, I had a prearranged interview with India's Prime Minister Nehru. Current Affairs wanted to use it but didn't want me in it! I was instructed to ask Nehru to pose my questions himself and then answer them — which instruction I of course ignored. But the newsroom at times was equally baffling. Soon after, in a second interview, Nehru revealed that China had just invaded India. I quoted him in an urgent cable to News, which I assume checked the wire agencies, found no confirmation, and spiked my exclusive report. Dismay over this swayed me to join Current Affairs' *Background* as host-reporter with regular contributors Alistair Cooke and Malcolm Muggeridge. The attraction was doing hour-long documentaries, but the program organization was hopeless and after one year I rejoined News as the first Far East correspondent, then was sent on to London.

Now Knowlton was seemingly in a position to end all the nonsense: News and Current Affairs would jointly produce an hour each Saturday and Sunday, and I was to be "Editor" of the News sections, making the most of the growing roster of correspondents. Given the effort at unity behind *Weekend*, I expected equal airtime, but early on the ruling was forty minutes Current Affairs, twenty minutes News. I didn't make an issue of this since weekends tend to be slim on news, yet occasionally for sure there would be a major news break. Finally, after endless production meetings overseen by Management appointee Ray Hazzan, I urged that if the News "Editor" deemed a situation to be of exceptional importance he should then have control of the entire hour.

The outcome was a three-page memo of demands from the two Current Affairs executives, Richard Nielson and Neil Andrews, signed by Nielson. It had me wondering what century they were in. For their requested team they listed twelve well-known males, "plus a girl."

The memo then proposed that Ray Hazzan "cease to have executive responsibility for the Series," that Current Affairs should "administer all the budget" and that "Mike be responsible to us rather than Ray." None of this was at all negotiable with me, nor I assumed with Knowlton, whose concept and authority was now so openly challenged.

For a very long day, I paced my hotel room opposite the Kremlin, waiting for a call that never came. What to do? It was no easy decision. I had implicitly given up my London correspondent role (Mariko remembers returning to Toronto with all our possessions in seventeen suitcases!). And for this new challenge the pay was far better! I realized that Knowlton would likely have all of Current Affairs — with its high-ranking management — on his back. He would be in salvage mode, but so was I.

After waiting two days I sent him a note saying I had no choice but to withdraw from the project because "… it is useless to have a concept which is viable and an executive team which is not." Knowlton called me right away. He needed a few days, he said, to sort things out. Would I please keep my decision strictly confidential until then, when I could return to my London post. He also wrote to me at the motel, expressing "… how saddened I am, because you still maintain such enthusiasm for the project and are aware of the importance of it.

"Please be totally assured that on a professional basis, aside from my personal admiration for you, your position has in no way been damaged and in fact has been enhanced in view of the manner in which you have conducted yourself in recent days. Thank you, Mike. Sincerely, Knowlton."

This was dated May 30, 1969. It was a generous letter considering that I hadn't invited further discussion, but then to have stayed on I would have let us both down.

I like to think that at times the subconscious takes charge, foreseeing other solutions, other challenges for the troubled conscious mind. I then had no inkling that a few weeks later I would get word from my Tokyo contacts, with whom Mariko had kept touch throughout my years in London, saying a press visa for filming in North Vietnam would be issued by mid- August (1969). I needed quick Toronto consent and at that point I wondered if Knowlton might think I'd known of the visa much earlier and so had sought to bow out of *Weekend*.

Perhaps that thought might explain his silence — the total silence of senior Management — on my documentary *Ho Chi Minh's People*. This most unusual silence, and the apparent screening of the film for some foreign entity, worried me for the entire flight to New York, where I had now to deliver the documentary to NBC.

NBC News: what a contrast! "Welcome," said producer Jerry Rosholt. "Hey, you must be some kinda hero up there."

"No," I laughed, "we don't have heroes — at least not at my network."

"Shame. Well, help us choose the excerpts — we're excited because we've got no idea what the reaction will be, but we'll sure let you know."

NBC's *Huntley-Brinkley* news found airtime in late December, 1969, for three consecutive excerpts, each four minutes, and Rosholt then wrote that he personally took the "first fifteen calls the final night and 4-of-5 were complimentary on your enterprise and our decision to air this series."

After the Hanoi saga, I took as much leave as possible. On March 28, I called the office to say I wouldn't be in for the usual early feed to Radio — my wife was already in labour.

"Well, Mike," said the News manager, "there's a good yarn on the wires. Germans selling tanks to Spain. Up to you, Mike."

I hung up. I still can't quite believe it!

CHAPTER NINE
The Network War

FOR A TIME, WITH the birth of our daughter Kyo (as in Tokyo), 1970 started as a blessed year, ridding me of such minor things as wars and networks, replaced by the most compelling cry of any: that of a newborn child. So in personal terms the preoccupation that is family greatly offset everything else. Despite a growing loss of confidence in Management, it was inconceivable that its lack of judgment would have the state network almost self-destruct — until it happened.

Until then, though there was much that dismayed me, I was never seriously discontented. I was starting my seventeenth year with the Network with no intention of ever leaving the Mother Corp!

Admittedly, when assigned to direct a documentary on Pierre Trudeau's tour of the Pacific Rim nations, I had zero enthusiasm, for it meant a month away from home on a politically polite film. Not my *genre* and not part of London's jurisdiction. But I was told that Knowlton had suggested the assignment, so I didn't argue. It seemed I was still the film guy, not realizing I was about to be the fall guy.

In Toronto for the edit, Knowlton summoned me in my role as president of the Foreign Correspondents Association. He looked bushed, none of the old buoyance, and bluntly stated that for budget reasons the Moscow bureau was to be closed imminently and the Hong Kong bureau would be phased out. There had been rumours of this, along with rumours that the newly launched *Weekend* was already bleeding money. Knowlton was adamant. He would not reconsider.

With the correspondents scattered around the world, fighting Management became a lonely task, but over the next few days we all signed off on a memo of protest which I had drafted. It stressed that "the quality and dimension of the News service and ultimately the Network's public image would be adversely affected" and that "political repercussions are clearly predictable. We genuinely believe that the closing of the Moscow bureau will be interpreted by the Soviet government as a hostile act by the Canadian government." And finally the memo emphasized that "these cutbacks will greatly increase our reliance on American network coverage" with Canadian audiences exposed more than ever to "the U.S. point of view."

For several days there was no response from Management. So we decided on crisis action. The memo was sent to President George Davidson, requesting his comment. Almost immediately, Davidson informed Knowlton he was coming to Toronto the next day and wanted a meeting of all concerned, a meeting I was asked to chair. The outcome was astonishingly swift.

In opening the meeting I said that everyone present had read the memo. There had been ample time for response, so now all that was needed was the opinion of the president. In less than a minute Davidson ruled that the investment in the foreign news bureaux was essential to the Network mandate and without further discussion he ordered that the proposed closures be rescinded.

It the stunned silence some thirty members of Management crowding the small conference room looked as if each had received a sudden sharp slap on the face! I caught a look of reproach from Knowlton, magnified by the heavy lenses he always wore. I left for London the next day, sensing that in saving two correspondent positions I had very likely endangered my own.

In terms of bureaucracy the Network Kremlin and the London bureau were little different. In size and pecking order it was like a small embassy. In the role of ambassador it had a "Representative" whose big day would be hosting his counterpart from big-daddy BBC, or selling some visiting MP on the bureau as the voice of Canada abroad. Once a week the representative, his secretary, and the bureau news managers, English and French, would meet to discuss priorities, such as space allotment, renovations, or which cocktail parties to attend. In my six years thus far as London correspondent I had never once been invited to the weekly meeting. The actual voice for the Canadian viewer or listener — the foreign correspondent — had absolutely no say in matters. But thankfully this cut both ways.

By some unwritten law, the correspondent never submitted ideas, let alone scripts, to the news manager, whose main function was commissioning freelance items and organizing the travel assignments suggested by the foreign correspondent or as ordered by the Toronto assignment desk. The only drawback was that in those days of costly phone calls it meant little or no direct communication between home base and the correspondent in the field. Assignments and story ideas were mostly routed through the bureau news manager, and this plus the time difference could cause serious disconnect.

Assigned to Israel early September, 1970, I was to discover the pitfalls of this second- to third-hand system of communication. On September 6, a militant faction known as the Fedayeen, which controlled the largest Palestinian refugee camp in Jordan, launched a surprise attack on the capital, Amman, and by cable I was ordered to get there. No one wanted to hear how unrealistic that was. There were no flights from Israel to Jordan or to any Arab country, so it meant routing to Athens, which I dutifully booked while fretting over the futility of it. The militants had seized Amman airport and had hijacked empty passenger jets of TWA, Swissair, and Pan Am, so no airline was getting in, nor wanted to!

For some ten days, the militants proved well-organized and well-armed, aided mainly by Syria, which even sent in tanks, while the U.S. dispatched the Sixth Fleet to the eastern Mediterranean. It was unarguably a big story, but its ending was very predictable. I tried persuading Toronto via London that Israel, prepared for a new war with Syria, was the bigger story. I knew that if Jordan's King Hussein couldn't repel the militants then Israel would; it would massively invade. I believed King Hussein's loyal Bedouin-led army would soon have all borders on lockdown and then would begin a grisly mop-up. I had spent time with King Hussein, a charming, soft-spoken man who readily agreed to pose for photos with my wife, but inwardly he was a man of steel. I had excellent contacts in Israel, dating to time spent with such legends as General Moshe Dayan and Prime Minister Golda Meir, so I suggested — and I suppose argued — that I stay in Israel and another crew could be sent somehow to Jordan.

The answer came via London in a terse cable ordering my immediate return there with further duties suspended, signed John Kerr, Area Head, News. A second cable from Peter Trueman, executive of the nightly TV news, confirmed the suspension but asked that I stay on a couple of days, which I did, to film conditions in the Israeli-controlled refugee camps in Gaza.

Trueman was new to the Network but well-versed in foreign affairs and seemed ready to listen; he was not part of the Management mindset and would soon become a victim of it. Kerr I'd never heard of but learned he was a former Current Affairs executive — and then I remembered seeing him at the Kremlin in an office next to Knowlton's. I knew that the Network could devise self-serving managerial titles faster than a revolving door. Even so, "Area Head" of News was news to me!

It was laughable yet troubling. It sounded like a Current Affairs take-over of News, but also my removal from the field and indefinite suspension just for stating how I read events was nonsensical — unless this was well-disguised payback for opposing Management on the bureaux affair some three months earlier, perhaps with my walkout from *Weekend*, and pressure from Washington over my North Vietnam coverage all thrown into the mix.

Whatever Management's motivation, this was war!

On leaving Israel September 20, I cabled Kerr "… cannot comprehend vindictive managerial action …" and by the time I arrived in London he had replied. "Your comments unwarranted and unacceptable. Awaiting your written explanation through Robbins …" So I cabled Robbie. "In complying with request for letter of explanation it is necessary to know what it is I am explaining; and what other factors influenced the action against me since Management has admitted there are other factors…."

It was certainly a war of words — would it escalate? Ron Robbins never did reply. Instead, Donald J. MacDonald, former deputy Chief News Editor but now retitled Supervisor of Information Resources, arrived in London to hand-deliver a letter which amounted to a verdict before any hearing. It stated that Management felt my "usefulness reduced" and my "services as a foreign correspondent would not be needed as of the New Year."

* * *

Up to then I thought there'd soon be a ceasefire. But sending Don to London with such a letter was not just a declaration of war — it was to be brutal. Don had been the network executive who'd hired me sixteen years before, so sending him ensured maximum salt in the wound!

We met at a small Italian restaurant where he handed me the letter. We had been close friends for all those years, always meeting at his home for dinner and chess whenever I was in Toronto. But watching me read the letter he showed not the slightest unease. This, almost as much as the letter, astonished me.

Though I had so often experienced Management's untroubled group-think, here was one of them executing orders even though his signature was almost certainly his only part in this charade. Reading it, I thought how different this was from the usual Management absurdities. It was totally destructive, for my career thus far and for the Network's investment in the millions of dollars for my travels reporting from some eighty countries.

And then, compounding matters, that other war was back in my life. A cable from Hanoi arrived at around the same time as Don.

It read: "Michael Maclear, CBC Canabroad London. Inviting you and Japanese crew visit Vietnam mid-December. Inform us your passport number, dates and way you take stop Ubavanhoa."

Hanoi's cable was a total surprise. I had not applied for another visa, and the "invitation" was unprecedented. What did it mean? I recalled my parting words to the Foreign Ministry contact, Tran, proposing we get access to the POW camps. But I couldn't guarantee Management such access, and, anyway, the inevitable controversy of such filming would make them nervous in the extreme. Yet Hanoi's cable called for a timely response. I was in no position to answer it — a correspondent about to be demoted, "usefulness reduced." Instead, I forwarded Hanoi's cable jointly to Ron Robbins, Knowlton Nash, and John Kerr. Briefly I considered revealing to Management my Hanoi contact so they could see how innocuous, how harmless the relationship was, but I never did.

* * *

(Forty-four years later, at Robarts Library checking on relevant archival material, I'm amused imagining Management's reaction had they known my primary connection with Hanoi.

I'm looking at a photo of Mariko and myself with Yasuo Yanagisawa visiting the small village of Mashiko, a two-hour train ride from Tokyo, a village where generation after generation of Japanese potters plied their craft. We had met Yanagisawa through Bob Nakai, a Visnews camera-man and lifelong friend. Through him I had met Mariko, who besides being an interpreter had a wide knowledge of Japanese ukiyo-e wood-cuts and pottery. Nakai knew everyone in Tokyo and suggested that if I wanted to get into China and North Vietnam I should meet Yanagisawa, a known communist who had just launched a new film agency, Nihon Denpa News, with offices in Peking (Beijing), Hanoi, and East Berlin.

The way Nakai set it up, Yanagisawa, Mariko and I would journey to Mashiko: there'd be no talk of politics, just pottery — a mutual fascin-ation which we'd thereafter share, together prowling the street pottery market at the Azabu-Juban district of Tokyo where Mariko and I lived after marrying in 1963. Yanagisawa never discussed his background or beliefs, which I gradually learned. Perhaps he saw in me a fellow spirit passionate about film and television. He too had started with the state broadcaster, NHK, becoming a wartime executive but secretly anti-war, and with the peace he joined Japan's outlawed Communist Party. Hounded into exile in China, he developed a close relationship with Mao's deputy and eventual prime minister, Zhou Enlai, and with the exiled, mystical Ho Chi Minh.

Yanagisawa and I never once discussed ideology, nor did I get the visas to Beijing and Hanoi that I sought while Far East correspondent; It was Mariko who kept touch with Bob Nakai and Yasuo Yanagisawa, meeting with them during her frequent London-Tokyo family visits. But how could I ever explain close human relationships to the Network!)

After a week waiting for Management's response to Hanoi's extraordinary invitation, I decided I would send them the "explanation" regarding Jordan they had demanded. Perhaps it would explain them to themselves and be a wakeup call. Dated September 24, 1970, it read like comic opera, my letter to them quoting their instructions:

"Early 17th, Mr. Gunning (News Manager, London) phoned me in Tel Aviv to say that I and my soundman, but not cameraman, were to proceed to Beirut, where we'd pick up a French Network cameraman.

"Evening, 17th, Mr. Gunning called, Montreal had refused use of their cameraman, so my sound recordist should, after all, remain in Israel. I was to proceed to Beirut alone. A *Weekend* camera crew was 'believed' to be in Beirut with their reporter Barry Callaghan. I was to use his crew.

"Late 17th, London not aware of any actual contact with Callaghan.

"17th, Toronto time. I called Peter Trueman, TV news Executive Producer, who said Mr. Callaghan's assignment 'did not call for him to report to News.' However, if I got into Amman and Callaghan was there, I 'would be able to use Callaghan's crew.' I said I doubted if this would be possible or welcome.

"Late 17th, Toronto time, 6:30 a.m., 18th my time, about to leave for the airport, I again call Trueman for any late news on Callaghan's where-abouts. I'm then casually told there was 'some displeasure' over my calls. I was now to stay put in Israel and 'I would hear further from John Kerr.'

"Morning, 18th, Gunning informed me I was being recalled to London but should stay in Israel another two days just in case...."

In summary, I pointed out that if News could not get the co-operation of Current Affairs regarding Callaghan, even though he was reporting for *Weekend*, the program supposed to bring the two sides together, what could I possibly do about it? They, though using the same offices, were obviously not talking to each other, yet I was to somehow get into Amman and *if* Barry Callaghan was there tell him to hand over his crew!

It was total farce and a huge waste of public money. I was hauled back to London while — as I'd suggested from the start — another crew with correspondent William Cunningham was sent to Beirut, a lush, calm watering hole at that time. They never did get into Jordan, where anyhow the uprising was being contained. A short time later, Egypt's President Anwar Sadat, who had maintained peace with Israel, was assassinated, and now, funds exhausted, the Network had no one in a very tense Israel — which had been the story epicentre all along.

Management never did reply to my "explanation." There was no meeting, no hearing on my coming demotion as a foreign correspondent. I wrote to Eugene Hallman, Head of English Broadcasting, who had praised my Prague coverage, then to his deputy Marce Monroe, rumoured as the puppet-master, then to Knowlton.

None of them answered, except for a second letter from Don Mac-Donald enlarging on the first: I could apply for a TV producer role but "we cannot make any guarantee."

Idling in London, it was clear that I was facing an organized silence by all senior management and that the tiff over Jordan couldn't possibly justify their action. It seemed they wanted everyone to know the extreme penalty for being a whistle-blower and going over their heads to the person ultimately responsible, the president. But even if their action against me was in any degree merited, their self-interest also showed a troubling disregard for the reason they held office: that of keeping the public informed. By now, Hanoi's cable had gone unanswered for a month and a Network management reared as always being right was about to self-destruct.

On October 16, 1970, with the kidnapping of a British diplomat James Cross by the FLQ — *Le Front de Liberation du Quebec*, an extremist minority — the Network reaction to Prime Minister Trudeau's evoking of the War Measures Act was instant, blanket self-censorship. Despite the sudden unleashing of armed troops everywhere in the capital, despite the passionate opposition in Parliament, Network management decided its duty (or its best self-interest) was to the government rather than to the public.

"CBC began censoring itself in what became the most shameful episode in its history," wrote columnist Morris Wolfe in *Saturday Night*. Though he stayed on at CBC until 1974, News executive Peter Trueman later described in his book *Smoke and Mirrors* being summoned by his superiors and told "We were to avoid commentary of any kind. We were told not to use man-in-the-street interviews or shoot film of any public demonstrations. We were to air no panel discussions on the October Crisis and to avoid reporting what the government was doing."

By December, with the FLQ crisis over, I tried again for a decision on Hanoi's "invitation," which understandably had lost any attention during the past several weeks. But now, into the very month Hanoi had specified for my filming and with no response for eight weeks, I felt I should send an apology and regrets. But first I called a highly placed friend, asking why the total disinterest on what could be major news — and I mentioned my hunch that the invitation was code for the first filming by a Western network of POW conditions.

"Really? That's big, but the bigger question for the Kremlin is you — or your affiliations. How come you got into Red China during Mao's Cultural Revolution, then into North Vietnam, then get *invited* back. You understand how they think?

"No, even they don't understand how they think. Okay, but it's no laugh — it's a journalist's job to get into such places."

"Of course, but right now the Kremlin has a three-man group checking up on you — they call themselves the *Troika*, ha ha."

I was stunned. "I better send Hanoi some polite excuse."

"Wait a few days," my friend said, "I have an idea."

CHAPTER TEN
That Other War

I ARRIVED IN MOSCOW — my first visit there — in mid-December, with two days to wait for the Aeroflot connection to Hanoi, two days touring one of the most winter-dismal cities I'd ever seen. I couldn't imagine living there, a sentiment which would later have great irony. But the immediate irony was that of a seasoned foreign correspondent being sent on a world exclusive assignment only to be dismissed immediately on his return!

Evidently, someone had let the American networks know of the Hanoi invitation (I wonder who that could have been!) and CBS and NBC right away started a bidding war for U.S. rights. For the Network to have backed off would have made it an international joke; for it to have even hinted that its reporter had some bias — or worse — would be indefensible. And anyway, the Network could now make a handsome profit, replenish the budget it had blown over Jordan, with all Hanoi costs being covered — all costs except mine! With a jobless New Year looming, Mariko and I had perforce abandoned London. Not knowing how long the Hanoi assignments would last, Mariko, with our daughter Kyo, just eight months old, had flown to Tokyo to be with family — this at our own expense.

This time I decided to fly to Hanoi with Aeroflot on the more secure northern route, yet to be bombed, but the unpressurized flying icicle made for a torturous journey. And surprisingly, my reception in Hanoi was no less frigid.

A "welcome" dinner for me and my Japanese camera crew turned quite ugly. Perhaps that cable from a colleague a year earlier about "hitting the jackpot" remained in their memory. Perhaps they needed to test me on that, because now the new head of the foreign relations committee, who had replaced Tran, launched into a tirade against Western journalists who "are unscrupulous mercenaries."

Angry, I rose to reply but felt cameraman Fujii's restraining grip on my arm. When the moment allowed I stood and bluntly told them this visit was personally costing me a great deal, more than they'd ever know, and whatever revenue my Network might make from my films they kept. "Look. I'm a journalist. The reward is being here, not the money." And I pulled out the empty lining of my trouser pocket. Then they laughed.

The next morning, Tran, now promoted at the Foreign Ministry, came to the hotel bearing a large packet of my favourite green tea as an olive branch. As he put it, the comments of the previous evening were "educational" and my visit was "timely." Tran said some "important" filming was still being discussed. In the meantime I would see significant changes if I revisited areas south of Hanoi. I thanked him but added what was important for Americans was seeing conditions in the POW camps.

"I know — be patient," he said as he poured more of the jasmine green tea which always seemed a great tranquillizer.

I would spend a week filming in the southern provinces closest to Hanoi. Like my travels here fifteen months earlier, what I witnessed was totally surprising and again totally unknown to the outer world. But where previously the landscape showed only death and devastation, now it gleamed with the bright red of bricks and tiles. New homes, schools, offices, and factories dotted the horizon, rising wherever the debris of bombed towns and villages had been cleared. Though I only travelled in three nearby provinces, this was revival seeded on a massive scale.

With the bombing pause now in its second year, and with "Vietnamization" accelerating the withdrawal of American troops from South Vietnam, the North in 1970 effectively aided the U.S. by slowing down the war and reducing the rate of troop infiltration, thus enabling a massive switch of military manpower for this new goal of rebuilding the home front. I learned that soldiers over fifty or those who had three or more years of combat, as well as all youth in their first year of conscription, were now drafted to the new priority of recreating urban life. In total, it involved some five hundred thousand troops. Either U.S. satellite intelligence had failed to detect all this, or — more likely — the Pentagon preferred to keep silent, as it had during the bombing years. But what if the bombing resumed? Then so would North–South troop infiltration.

This was big news, and like my previous visit I again wondered why I was being allowed to film all this, since obviously the American public would now learn of it and Washington might then retaliate.

The response I repeatedly heard was, "For as long as we can we must rebuild industry and living conditions to enable protracted war." The threat of *protracted war* was not what the U.S. public wanted to hear.

Our films would show a society dramatically revitalized. Along the banks of the receding Red River, near the town of Thai Binh, a mile-long army of five thousand reassigned men, with only the most primitive equipment, laboriously rerouted the river to create canals to serve new homes and offices at the city's edge, while other men and women, using only bare hands, shaped blocks of mud for the factories producing mountains of bricks that lined the streets-to-be. At siesta, despite the wintry weather, everyone just lay on the mud banks for two hours sleep, accompanied by the improbable sight of a young woman in traditional dress standing on a platform of caked mud, singing some ancient folk song.

But the appeal now went beyond nationalist sentiment. Cash bonuses were one reward for exceptional productivity, and civilian volunteers were also guaranteed a substantial extra rice ration. As the rebuilding spread to the more rural regions, the incentives were ever more galvanizing: ownership of a two-room brick home could be bought for the equivalent of U.S. $500.

This was still five years income for the average worker in the North, but during wartime enforced austerity many families had saved that much.

For others a room in new worker's "condos" could be rented for pennies — again, based on your productivity. Swiftly, the caves that had been home during the "second resistance war," as the U.S. bombing was called, had largely emptied, but remained cared for just in case. A great many cave-factories had now moved to nearby two-storey brick buildings, I was told. There was boasting of a "New North." Yet although morale had rocketed, everyone I talked to openly feared the future, which for Hanoi was to prove horrific.

* * *

Returning to Hanoi, we were all in good spirits. Our film would make news, and I was ready to fly home, but a message came summoning us to Tran's office at the Foreign Ministry. First he said that an interview had been arranged with Premier Pham Van Dong for later that day — and then the news I had hoped for. We were to be allowed filming of a POW camp and interviews with two or three captive American pilots. It would be in two days' time.

"But that's Christmas Day!" I exclaimed.

"Yes, early morning, but there's a flight later that day to Vientiane connecting to Hong Kong–Tokyo. You may just make Christmas dinner with your family!"

He was smiling and I can't remember ever smiling so much. For a journalist, what a Christmas gift! But then, in stern voice, Tran began to list strict rules for the filming. No physical contact, no conversation with the prisoners. The interviews would be limited to four questions which he needed to know now, so the American pilots would have advance notice and accept or decline.

I decided the simpler the questions the easier it would be for the POWs, and I wrote them down for Tran: (1) Name, rank, when and where shot down, after how many missions, their family details; (2) What parcels and letters do you regularly receive, what do they contain, and how often can you write home? (3) Describe your daily routine, work, duties, your meals, recreation, exercise — and health; (4) Do you talk to each other about the war; what are your feelings on this, what might you want to say directly to the American people ?

Tran read the questions without comment. I asked him, "May I cable my network and NBC to prepare for this film?"

He nodded then gently said, "So this is goodbye. Who knows if we'll meet again, but you have been fair in your reports and you will always be welcome in Vietnam."

Of course, in my interview with Premier Dong (for which advance questions were not required) the discussion was almost wholly about the POWs.

Coinciding with my arrival in Hanoi, a list of 368 American pilots said to be held in the North, giving their full names and rank, had been released at the Paris peace talks — the first such information on the captives. But Washington had reacted negatively, still insisting that of the approximately 1,500 Vietnam MIAs, most were likely being held in the North.

So I asked the premier, "Does the list of prisoners names just released mean there are no other prisoners in North Vietnam?"

He replied, "That was the full and complete list," including the names of twenty who had died in captivity, and the prime minister added, "It was a humanitarian gesture to the families of these men."

When pressed that the U.S. maintained there were many more prisoners than listed, Dong became angry. "The Nixon people are scoundrels, really scoundrels, to talk of this; it is they who show no humanitarian concern by talking like this."

"How is the U.S. to know the condition of the prisoners?"

The prime minister responded emotionally. "We Vietnamese know all too well what it is like being prisoners — under the French. Ask the Americans in our camps. I swear to you these men are well treated."

At 7 a.m. on Christmas Day 1970, our jeeps arrived but without our usual minder, Lam, and without interpreter Vu. Instead, two armed military officers scrutinized our equipment and then, once in the jeeps, Fujii, Ishigaki, and I were firmly blindfolded. The drive lasted some ten minutes, but with all the twists and turns of the Hanoi streets, I quickly lost any sense of direction. Only the ever-honking traffic confirmed that we were still in a well-populated area of Hanoi. Then, having entered the prison grounds, our blindfolds were removed.

Our regular fixer, Lam, with his palm up-down, yes-no language, was waiting for us. The first "No" was our attempt to film the fifteen-foot prison walls and guard towers. From what I could see, the POW camp consisted of only five single-storey buildings grouped around a spacious grassy area which had as a centrepiece a concrete-lined pond overhung by willow trees. Near one building we were led to, the doorway was just a high latticed bamboo curtain. Beside it, there was an exercise yard where, obviously expecting us, seven captive pilots were playing basketball. This we filmed, but no conversation was allowed except for each of them stating his name and rank.

(So many decades later, with the ever constant help of Brock Silversides, I am anxiously searching my archival records. Of many thousands of news reports for the Network, I seldom kept copies unless the subject matter had major historical value, so it was a relief to find the original script for the POW filming as well as my scrawled filming notes, proof that I had fully emphasized the limitations. The script began:

> Behind the bamboo curtain a row of six rooms fronting a long verandah. Filming was rigidly restricted to this sector…. The rooms, despite the window bars and door bolts, were hardly cells. Twenty foot wide by twelve, each had three beds, though only two to a room were made up. Two blankets on each. Family pictures adorned some rooms. Books were generally evident. Certainly clean, well-kept but the genuine article? … Depending on how many men share these rooms there could be upwards of sixty prisoners here.
> "Lavishly decorated with yuletide messages, I saw a communal hall where on Christmas Eve a (different) Japanese cameraman from Nihon Denpa News filmed about thirty prisoners, eating and carol-singing. But I saw only seven men. Of course, the brief glimpse of only seven men cannot be presented as a clear overall picture….)

* * *

For the interviews we were taken to a room where the sight of a large Christmas tree with twinkling bulbs seemed improbable, clashing with the iron bars on the single window. Instead of the beds seen in other rooms, a small table had been brought in — two chairs on one side, just one chair for me facing the two prisoners (and facing the troubling twinkling Christmas bulbs!)

Camera loaded, we waited several minutes, then the tension suddenly heightened. The first person to enter the room, accompanied by an armed soldier, brought instant memories of alarm: it was Vien, the hostile minder who had hindered and cursed me on that journey fifteen months earlier through the devastated southern provinces. His appearance here could only mean he'd been chosen as the most aggressive watchdog.

He showed no sign of recognition of the crew or me. He merely approached as close as possible, snarling, "These are the rules. You may only ask the questions you submitted, no supplementary questions, no con- versation of any kind with the prisoners, no physical contact whatsoever. Do you understand?"

"Yes, I understand." I wanted no argument. This would be the first time a Western broadcast journalist had a recorded interview with captive pilots, whose fate and condition had been largely unknown for as long as five years. Nothing must derail this interview, as it easily could if Vien found a way. I was tense. Not least, I naively thought this filming might help bring an end to the war — and to my war!

I'd been told that all seven Americans we had filmed exercising were prepared to be interviewed, but only two would be allowed — which two I didn't know. To avoid any contact, I was already seated when they entered the room: Robert James Schweitzer, thirty-eight, and Walter Eugene Wilber, forty, both U.S. navy commanders and both from Pennsylvania, both married with two sons.

They took their seats without any greeting, clearly well briefed on the rules, and the interview began. I was surprised at how composed they were, how relaxed when they spoke.

Four questions could go by quickly, so when they dried up on the first I stalled on the second question, instead with raised eyebrow looking from one to the other of them until they caught on and began talking some more. So it went for almost twenty minutes. I was allowed to take notes. Their day began at sunrise, three meals a day, then the routine of cleaning their rooms, then exercise, "volleyball and other sports." They were allowed to send and receive letters once a month, also at Christmas and special occasions like Mother's Day.

"We read a great deal," Wilber said, mentioning among the books they were given *Vietnam! Vietnam!* and *Vietnam: The Unheard Voices.* But there were occasionally also non-contentious films, Schweitzer saying he had just seen a production of Shakespeare's *Twelfth Night*.

On the final question, "What are your feelings on the war?" both were forceful.

"We discuss the war very much because the war is very close to us here. We've talked about it a lot, how we feel. We are all involved," said Schweitzer, adding, "I know I've had the deepest discussions I've ever had in my life with fellow prisoners here and we've had to go to the very core of our feelings on a number of things — loyalty, what is it, where does it lie. Morality, legality."

And Wilber cut in, saying, "This war is wrong. The answer is that this war must be ended, must be stopped, now. Once we do that the Vietnamese can solve their own problems."

They had been given all four questions two days earlier — a lot of time to weigh and agree on their stance and sentiments. Despite the rules, at the end Wilber leaned across the table, extending his hand, and without a thought I shook it.

Once the two of them had left, Vien went ballistic. I was one of the enemy, a fraud, a liar, a swine, he screamed over and over, louder and louder. I saw Fujii clutching the camera to his chest, probably fearing as I was that Vien might try to seize our precious film!

So loud was Vien's uproar that — as happened on the original confrontation — Lam, with an extra military guard, came running. Hearing about the handshake, he looked at me with disapproval but quickly took control. "Most unfortunate," he told me. "You knew the rules," then to Vien, "Mr. Maclear is leaving Vietnam in a few hours, which would seem to settle matters."

I always felt some tug leaving Vietnam, though mainly at that time in leaving Fujii and Ishigaki, two of the finest, dearest people I'd ever worked with. But soon I was on the plane, typing on my much-travelled Royal a lengthy article on the POW filming.

At Vientiane airport, I found a public phone and, feeling ridiculous, asked the operator for a collect call to the foreign desk of the *New York Times* in New York. There was a grunt, much crackling and what sounded like the entire Pacific Ocean hurtling my way, and then a calm voice:

"Foreign Desk." Before leaving for Vietnam I had prepared the *Times* for such a call, with an embargo on the copy until the film also reached New York and Toronto. Now, over an ancient phone at a dysfunctional airport in the remotes of Asia, I clearly heard "Just give us everything you've got." It was unreal, uncanny, beyond all odds.

In Tokyo, still late Christmas Day, I reunited with my family, then on Boxing Day at the NBC studio with the film edited and readying the satellite feed to Toronto and New York, unreality returned. It was like hearing from two different planets.

"We're clearing the air for this," the New York producer said excitedly.

"We can only take maybe six minutes for *Weekend*," said the Toronto producer.

"You must have one helluva story already," the NBC Tokyo producer responded.

"Yeah, we've got a Malcolm Muggeridge special on the life of Jesus."

"Christ, that story is two thousand years old!"

"Ha, ha. Tell Maclear he's to get back here right away, for the correspondents' year-end review."

It was like hearing, "Never mind Vietnam — you've got a war on your hands over here, buddy." At that the countdown really hit me: my role as a foreign correspondent was to end with the new year — in just five days' time!

It seemed such an ironic ending. *Weekend* was the Sunday show I'd walked away from the year before over this very issue that News should control the program if there was a major news break — and the first recorded POW interviews were just that. Muggeridge's timeless film essays I had directed during my year with *Background*, where the makeshift organization had driven me back to News. But clearly Current Affairs had now prevailed.

For a network under fire for its blundering over the War Measures Act just weeks earlier, well, by Jesus, ancient history was sure safer!

In contrast, NBC was "clearing the air," and in a most unusual arrangement both NBC and CBS would air a prime-time news special almost simultaneously.

But my own network seemed to me displeased by it all. Now I sensed that I was needed back for the foreign correspondents gathering as a warning to them all, a kind of public hanging!

I still had no idea what, if any, News position I might be given. But for five more days I was still bound by a contract that had me working any day, any hours, if so ordered. Rather than give Management any valid reason for its actions, I got a flight December 28 to Toronto, to that other still-escalating war!

CHAPTER ELEVEN
No Ceasefire

WHAT FOLLOWED WAS BOTH heartening and dismaying. NBC on Sunday, December 27 had devoted major resources to the POW footage. A young Tom Brokaw had been assigned to watch the film live with the family of navy Commander Walter Wilber. NBC had followed up with viewer reaction, which overwhelmingly favoured any information after years of uncertainty as to the fate of captive pilots, some of them prisoners for more than six years. The NBC special went to air just after 9 p.m. on the 27th, with the POW interviews running seventeen minutes, and the CBS report titled "U.S. Prisoners Speak" ran parallel — four times as much coverage as that used by my own network, as listed on their archives.

I had arrived in Toronto on the 28th, too late to see any of the POW footage on air, but in time for the fallout! Significantly, the report I had filed from Laos dominated the front page of the *New York Times*, with not a word changed. Together with photos of the POWs filmed, it spread over four columns on the front page and another ten columns inside. A separate dispatch contained my interview with Pham Van Dong on prisoner conditions. Along with additional articles on North Vietnam's defiant rebuilding, the *Times* articles had been syndicated to thirty prominent world newspapers, including the London *Times*, *Die Welt*, *La Figaro*, *Asahi Shimbun*, and the *Herald-Tribune (International)*, as well as scores of leading U.S. regional papers.

Significantly, the *Times* seemingly gave little credence — a short summary at the very end of my dispatch — to official reaction following the NBC and CBS broadcasts. An unnamed government spokesperson had taken a dismissive approach, saying the two prisoners filmed were among a small group of POW previously interviewed by "other reporters" (Swedish and Japanese) and "Mr. Maclear got the standard treatment" — thus ignoring the fact that for the first time *recorded* interviews with American POWs had received prominence on major American media. And with the *Times* following up the TV networks, the Nixon Administration found itself in full denial mode.

At a specially arranged press conference — filmed by the networks — Secretary of Defense Melvin Laird flatly stated that the film was "a carefully staged production" and that the POW camp filmed was a known "show camp" which his aides jokingly called the "Hanoi Hilton," a nickname which would become a household word, though as misleading as everything else that Laird and the White House had to say. At a separate White House briefing, press secretary Ronald Ziegler stated that President Nixon regarded the permitted filming as "total disregard of the terms of the Geneva convention" (a dubious notion given that Vietnam was an undeclared war), and as quoted by UPI, Nixon accused Hanoi of "a barbaric and inhuman attitude" towards the POWs.

Off the record, the White House spin was "the Canadian was deceived" and then deceived became "duped."

Only a month before, in "Operation Kingpin," six helicopters from the Seventh Fleet had attempted a midnight rescue of POWs from a camp at Son Tay, west of Hanoi, only to find the camp entirely empty. So, given that embarrassment, both Pentagon and White House intelligence on the Vietnam War was becoming increasingly doubted.

But not by the Network!

In the Vietnam War's final years, the fate and release of the captive Americans became the primary factor for any peace agreement. So for Hanoi to have planned a "staged production" at a "show camp," which if proven would be certain to further damage the peace negotiations, made no sense — to my mind, at least! Considering all this, Washington's response to the POW film was exceptionally deceitful.

Wartime politics might justify official Washington to bluster and even knowingly lie; nothing justified the Network leaning Washington's way.

The day after the Melvin Laird press conference, Network management ordered me to answer the Nixon-Laird charges on a hastily devised daytime, live television program.

I know of no precedent where a major Network, without itself first seeking clarification from its correspondent, succumbed so readily to a foreign government attack.

Perhaps to lend the questioning an air of authority that viewers might find more convincing, one of the foreign correspondents, rather than a staff announcer, was detailed to pose the question, "Were you duped?"

To have refused to partake in the charade would only imply that I had my own doubts — which I did not. I spoke about the familiarity with the camp that the prisoners had shown, noting that Wilber knew how to find a hidden window latch when the heat of the camera lights necessitated fresh air, or when Schweitzer stressed "we are close to the war here" — meaning the years of Rolling Thunder which reached close to them on the fringes of Hanoi. I stressed that a reporter, while citing the restrictions, must learn whatever possible — otherwise our audience learns nothing.

Looking up at the studio control room, I could see the shadows of watching Management, perhaps the Troika ready to pull the plug if I criticized the Network publicly. Pointedly, I stressed that ignorance or denial of the facts was the making of overall destructive wars! And clearly my war with the Network (or its with me) was still escalating, for this live cross-examination showed how little they cared about my North Vietnam reportage, other than the dollars.

But regardless of how management felt about the war, or about me, the seeming rush to side with Nixon-Laird, *despite the positive reaction of U.S. viewers*, can be rated high on the Network's list of lows. There had been no pressure, no clear reason for such a public grilling — other than an opportunity, perhaps, for further vengeance for my having opposed Management over its proposed foreign bureaux closings.

Their action was soon to backfire. The feedback I got was concern that if the Network could seemingly disavow its own long-time correspondent for no proven reason, then it would invite public doubt on the validity of the Network as a whole.

But aside from this, there was tangible unease over Management's autocratic methods, by which News clearly fared the worst. The foreign correspondents were abruptly told this would be the last year for the traditional year-end gathering. None of us then knew that Phil Calder was soon to be recalled after just a short spell as Bonn-based correspondent, while David Levy (Moscow) was also soon gone, by choice or not we never knew.

In a notable loss to the Network, William Cunningham (Far East), who for many years had been a kind of torch-bearer keeping us all in touch, would decamp to Global television, as eventually would Peter Trueman to become Global's news anchor, while Tom Gould (former Far East) had already quit to be Director, News and Current Affairs, at CTV.

The world of Canadian television news was rapidly changing — if the Network but knew it! Looking back, the *Canadian Journal of Communication* in a survey titled "Coverage of the Vietnam War in an Organizational Context," published by Simon Fraser University, referred to "the feeling within CBC management that reporters given too much head might become too combative, might embarrass the Corporation" to the extent where it led to "censoring yourself."

As a result, in the case of Vietnam, "U.S. Networks showed longer versions of Maclear's reports than were seen in Canada," and the review then quoted "senior newsman" Bill Cunningham that "Maclear's feeds were very heavily scrutinized and cut and hacked because they were quite different from the conventional wisdom being reported at the time."

Yet nearing New Year, 1970, I felt absurdly docile. I was no longer London Correspondent — nor officially anything else — but even so, I still had to complete the production of an hour documentary titled *North Vietnam Revisited* while ceaselessly pondering what options, if any, I had.

Then Management began to have second thoughts, kind of. Early January I got a call from John Kerr suggesting we meet at the motel coffee lounge. He didn't bother with pleasantries or coffee, he just stood, saying, "We're pleased you didn't go to the president this time, so we're prepared to give you another foreign correspondent posting. You'll hear further." And then he left. Why the "Area Head" bothered to cross the street for this first person-to-person encounter I have no idea.

But the follow-up from Management was hardly a ceasefire. When I learned of the new posting I could almost hear the derisive laughter echoing through the Kremlin. It was to be Moscow!

A few days later, January 8, 1971, a letter from Don MacDonald stated only that his earlier letter of October 27 dismissing me as a foreign correspondent "is now rescinded."

A separate letter from him — on the same January 8 date — stated: "I wish to advise you that later this month you will be suspended for five days without pay. This decision has been taken after a careful inquiry ... surrounding your assignment in the Middle East last September. It was felt that your attitude was a hazard to effective coverage of News....."

By now, the Management mindset warranted an in-house psychiatrist. The contradictions were baffling, the idiocy and pound-of-flesh approach unchanging. If I were really a "hazard" to News, and they could prove it, then they had a duty to fire me right away!

The only thing clear to me then was that in terms of my future the Network Management still could not be trusted. On January 16, a third letter from MacDonald formally confirmed "It is the Corporation's intention to transfer you from your present post to that of Moscow Correspondent later this year."

In one devilish move they had heeded the president's ruling of keeping the bureau open while in effect saying, "You wanted to keep Moscow — now you've got it!" Compounding the insincerity (and their defiance of their president) the posting was to be for radio only, with no camera crew. So much for the Network's seventeen-year investment in the "film guy"!

I did not respond. I called Mariko to get back to London, where we'd talk things over, since we'd be there anyway for a few more months, or until any move to Moscow. I certainly didn't want this posting, but it was a job at the same pay. And perhaps I could persuade them to hire a camera crew.

On the 17th, with a copy of *North Vietnam Revisited*, I flew to New York, as I had the previous year, to deliver the documentary to NBC. On the plane, reading the *Globe and Mail*, I was astonished to find in the entertainment section a short item headlined "Maclear Suspended Without Pay." Management had actually issued a press release, with the penalty commencing the next day when the documentary was to air!

So now I was heading to New York, unpaid, to ensure the Network could collect a fat fee from my work. On the plane, I made a belated New Year resolution — quit.

* * *

Back in London there was a letter from Knowlton, dated January 18, 1971, the night the documentary aired. On CBC letterhead, it said: "Dear Michael: After all the shouting and noise has simmered down, I simply wanted to say that I felt the North Vietnam documentary was a particularly good one … it was a damn fine piece of broadcast journalism of which you should be proud. Best personal regards, Knowlton."

That was the only comment on the program by anyone in Management and the only note from Knowlton during the past agonizing four months, this from the Director of News and Public Affairs, so who if anyone was calling the shots? How to make sense of it — my being a "hazard" to the News and also a "damn fine" journalist"?

"After all the shouting …" Was that how simply they regarded the intended ruin of my career at the Network over a disagreement when I was already in a war zone, a matter which couldn't possibly explain Management's gross overreaction?

Yet I did feel that Knowlton, however sidetracked he'd become, was trying to say "I'm sorry."

In London, I was given no assignments, no duties, no date for the supposed transfer to Moscow, on which I had never even verbally agreed. The plus side was more time with Mariko and Kyo. But in such total limbo, confidence wanes, self-doubt becomes mental torture. Had I been too openly critical of Management? As a "good" journalist had I been too sympathetic to North Vietnam's suffering?

A "hazard" to news coverage — for a reporter there could be no more serious charge than that, and they were getting away with it! I had no means or money to legally challenge them. A "hazard" to the News? Did others share that verdict? I found myself reaching for the reviews, which until then I'd never had time to read. On both documentaries, NBC and Toronto's impartial PR had forwarded viewer response received by phone calls and letters. Now I turned to these as my jury.

I started with the letter from NBC's news producer Jerry Rosholt, who had excerpted *Ho Chi Minh's People*. By his personal count of callers right after the broadcast, 80 percent were "complimentary." But he disclosed that NBC's *First Tuesday* series, which initially planned to run the entire documentary, had at the last moment decided not to, and Rosholt wrote: "Most of us on *Huntley-Brinkley*, after viewing your entire hour, felt that it should be shown in its entirety.... None of us agreed with the decision of the producer of *First Tuesday*, and others, not to use any of it."

Clearly, Mr. Rosholt was in no danger of becoming a "hazard" for having an opinion!

On the subsequent *North Vietnam Revisited*, NBC mail was only 60 percent in favour. In Canada, press reviews for *Ho Chi Minh's People* were overall unanimously in favour. Examples:

" ... an absolutely superlative documentary." — Bob Blackburn, *Toronto Telegram*;

"... Maclear's success with this film ... is the incomparable evidence of the destruction wreaked by U.S. bombs. It is a unique document" — Leslie Millin, *Globe and Mail*;

"... the documentary is the most trustworthy and informative presentation to come out of North Vietnam...." — James Spears, *Vancouver Province*

Of the first batch of seventeen viewer letters, only two disapproved, one calling me "a dirty, rotten communist hireling."

Of the initial batch for the second documentary, the ratio was a close ten-to-six supportive. Typical of the former, Eldon of Kindersley, Saskatchewan, wrote, "Thank you very much. News reporting by the CBC is by far the most value I get from listening and viewing," and typical of the latter, Mr. E.S. of Kenora, Ontario, wrote, "As a Canadian taxpayer I strongly object to communist propaganda broadcasts over CBC."

My favourite of them all, from D.W. of Picton, Nova Scotia, was really what I was looking for — some advice for the moment: "Dear Sirs: That long streak of misery you have in South East Asia would be better for himself, and for the Canadian public in general, if he went home and got a little home cooking."

Well, D.W. of Picton, Nova Scotia, I was going to take your advice. I resolved to forget the television news business for a time and just stay home — and by the way, D.W., Mariko was proving a master chef!

What I really got from the various reviews was clarity on where my duty as a journalist was ultimately owed — not to the Network, nor to some governing authority, nor to the patriotism of the moment, rather to those names in the letters I'd read — to the viewing public. What I needed to do, I decided, was move on and abandon the Network as bad news!

On a sudden impulse, I phoned Tom Gould at CTV, saying "Tom, do you need a London correspondent?"

Laughing, he said, "Mike, we don't have *any* foreign correspondents."

An hour or so later he called back, saying "You're on!"

The planning required time and secrecy. With my CBC pension refund we'd finally own a home. CTV would help out by partly renting it as their office. The timing was just right — for a mere 19,000 pounds (then $50,000) we found a small but charming Georgian row house on New King's Road, the poor man's Chelsea, and our new life began.

In late May, 1971, in Toronto to formally sign on as CTV's first foreign correspondent, I made a last nostalgic visit to the bar opposite the Kremlin, my letter of resignation in my pocket, ready to hand it over after a courage-enhancing Bacardi and Coke. Or maybe it was two or three!

Word got around and old friends came by, joined at one point by Peter Trueman. He sensed what was happening and said (and I paraphrase), "Look, I know you don't want Moscow — how about a producer job right here?"

As News executive producer, Trueman probably didn't have authority to hire me without senior management approval, so he had to be confident — not that it mattered, for the Bacardi had done its work. I was definitely out. But the Bacardi also had me saying, "Put it in writing," and Trueman did, scrawling an offer on a paper coaster, which I kept as a souvenir.

It read: "CBC. May 28/71. Dear Michael: This is to confirm that it is our intention to bring you back to Toronto to a suitable position in which you'd be guaranteed a minimum of $20,000 per annum for two years with a supplementary contract of $2,000 on your base pay for the first year. Peter Trueman, Head, CBC TV News."

Trueman had been frontman in the "shouting" over Jordan, and he throughout had seemed sympathetic. And for months the "Area Head" had been out of the picture, as least in my case, so a ceasefire might have been possible.

But the absurdity was no less. After four months of Management silence as to Moscow or some alternative, on a surprise visit that triggered

Trueman's initiative, I was being offered a sensible role at 30 percent more than my current salary — not that it mattered.

All that mattered was delivering my resignation, the yearning to be rid of the Kremlin and the Troika and Management's muddled mind. It was just a five-minute walk to the CTV offices on Charles Street East. Such a short walk to tomorrow that I wondered why it had taken me so long.

CHAPTER TWELVE
Deadly Intent

THE IMMEDIATE DIFFERENCE WAS CTV's eagerness for me to return to North Vietnam if at all possible. The private network was then owned by a handful of regional affiliates and run by a sparse group of departmental managers. Unlike the fiefdoms at the state network, CTV's managers reported directly to the network president. And with Tom Gould as director of both News and Current Affairs there was none of the nonsensical rivalry and wasteful duplication that I had been encountering at the "Mother Corp." I had been there seventeen years, but as I had told Mariko, "The next seventeen years should be better."

And from the start they were. Though I would be with CTV just seven years, it was a highly creative time. Tom Gould's approach was to woo the best journalistic talent he could persuade, then — spared from countless bosses — give them largely free rein. Soon after I joined CTV, so did the incomparable Craig Oliver, then Lloyd Robertson among the swelling number who made that walk up Jarvis Street to Charles Street East, where management and staff shared the same meagre premises.

For me it was to prove a rapid advance as a television journalist-producer. After the first year, Gould expanded the London bureau, adding the highly professional Peter Kent — and later Henry Champ — to take over daily news coverage so that I was freed for the hour-long flagship *W5*.

But at first there was no staff, no secretary or researcher or assignment organizer or logistics manager, not even a bookkeeper. So my new assignment of providing a weekly ten-minute events feature, with all the travel involved, was near impossible. But it led to the weekly prime-time half-hour *Maclear*, short documentaries filmed worldwide and billed as "personal journalism." It started with a million-plus audience — a rating for the most part sustained for four years.

At CTV ratings were the blood of existence, whereas the state network received what grew to a billion-dollar-a-year government subsidy. In part, ratings explained Tom Gould's urging that I return to Hanoi. The private network was not in the least concerned about controversy, which within bounds it relished — attention spelled ratings. But Tom also had a personal reason; for CBC he had spent a great deal of time in South Vietnam, coinciding with my first entry into the North, and he understood that 'Nam was the story of the sixties, whatever one's opinion of the war.

From the start, his sentiments on the war would be quite the opposite of mine, but he never let this interfere with the priority of first-hand reporting of the news. It was this that made Tom — and CTV — a standout during those years.

In truth, I then had no desire at all to return to North Vietnam. My two previous wartime visits had been personally very costly, leading — as I saw it — to a distrustful management smarting from being overruled on the foreign bureaux affair, contriving a vengeful destruction of my career with the Network.

But on joining CTV I once more applied to Hanoi for a press visa. For some fifteen months there was no response, except for a somewhat critical cable from my main contact, Denpa News president Yasuo Yanagisawa, dated September 12, 1972, saying, "We received some opinions from Vietnam side about a part of your news articles after your previous visit to Hanoi. Please deal with your news articles carefully." This was the only time my good friend had expressed any comment of any nature on my reportage, and given the vague wording so typically Japanese I still had no idea, nor cared much what in my syndicated articles had offended Hanoi. Presumably it was some observation on the Christmas Day, 1970, filming at the POW camp, which had equally upset Washington.

Oh well, for a war correspondent pleasing neither side is how it should be!

But then just a few days later a second cable routed through Denpa said a press visa was granted for the period of October. My first reaction was why now? Except for the formal Paris peace talks — year after year of mere testing each other — and the equally going-nowhere so-called "secret talks" between U.S. Secretary of State Henry Kissinger and Hanoi's senior delegate Le Duc Tho, the Vietnam War had settled into total stalemate and relative inertia. The only new element in late 1972 was just *how* the voting that November would impact the war, with Richard Nixon likely to be re-elected president. My second reaction: this time, no more Moscow — I'd take the Laos route!

Arriving in Hanoi back at the Thong Nhat Hotel with Denpa's Fujii-san and Ishigaki-san again assigned to me, there was a noticeable tension that hadn't filtered out to the Western media. From my room, for the first time at the Thong Nhat, I saw a somehow familiar sight of black-clad, rife-armed teams practicing urban guerrilla warfare on the hotel roof — familiar because after a while I recognized the kitchen staff and our long-time waitress, now all dodging behind chimneys, AKs pointing at imagined American paratroops while in the distance sirens sounded. It was unexpected and seemed unrealistic, but then I learned that part of the hotel basement was being reinforced as an air raid shelter for guests, and, certainly significant, at dinner over the same-old, same-old chicken that night, Fujii revealed that large numbers of older civilians and children, upwards of a third of Hanoi's non-essential population, had recently been evacuated north of the city. "Much people gone," as he succinctly put it.

I remembered how on my first visit to the North three years earlier I'd constantly been told, "The bombers will return," but then a year later finding an almost carefree mood as the southern provinces began rapid rebuilding of homes and factories. Fujii, through Denpa's Hanoi contacts, had heard of renewed U.S. naval air attacks immediately south of Hanoi. So the next day I asked interpreter Vu, assigned to us again with minder-coordinator Lam, to arrange filming on the southern outskirts of Hanoi.

We began on October 10th, filming "filler" material: working life, housing, outdoor food markets, but with no sign or sound of U.S. aircraft.

The next day, October 11, filming around the lunch hour near the same outdoor market, the sudden scream of jet fighters stunned us all, not least because it came from the least likely place — the very centre of

Hanoi. Seconds later, scanning the skyline, Fujii with his camera raised, I saw two low-flying jets — or perhaps three, because there was a third thunderclap — making what had to be a second pass of the city centre. And then, in a flash, a mere blink of the eye, it seemed two giant black-birds fell from the sky.

We had just witnessed the first-ever bombing of Hanoi. For eight years of U.S. combat Hanoi had been ruled strictly off limits. Could it be pilot error? Certainly not based on what we had seen. Sky-jocks defying orders? Possibly. Or a dangerous escalation of the war? I asked Fujii "Did we get it?" and he rolled his eyes.

"Far off, maybe."

Though he had switched to wide-angle, we were at least a mile distant from the attack; at best we'd have hazy dots on film. And possibly nothing very serious had occurred.

We had to find out, fast. I turned to Lam. "Let's get there, we must hurry."

But he flatly refused, saying, "We need permission." Permission? How?

This couldn't be happening — here in the epicentre of war there was no communication. No one had a phone!

Lam wouldn't even agree to our returning to our hotel. He was highly agitated, with Vu quoting him that he didn't know what had happened, or what might happen next, but that it was his duty to protect us! Finally, he agreed to send our driver to the Foreign Ministry for information and instructions. So began a three-hour wait as frustrating as anything I can remember.

When the driver returned he spoke excitedly to Lam. "What is he saying?" I asked.

Lam replied, "He's saying we must hurry!"

What we saw next was perhaps the most ironic twist of the entire Vietnam War. Having largely financed the last years of the French colonial war with the Viet Minh, and having then taken up the war that France abandoned, the U.S. in its first bombing of Hanoi had destroyed all that actively remained of the French era.

The U.S. fighter jets had very likely followed the broad central boulevard known as Embassy Row, which led to the heart of Hanoi:

Ba Dinh Square. Nearing it, the French consulate — then known as the French Mission — had taken a direct hit. When we arrived there some three hours after the attack, the relief effort had only just begun. Perhaps the priority need to alert all Hanoi's defenses explained the delay. But as we began filming the dead and injured were still being pulled from the rubble.

In a compound of three buildings the main one had been largely levelled, the others shattered, with the blast also ripping through neighbouring embassies. For the camera, I stood atop the rubble to describe the scene as both the French staff and the equally unprepared Vietnamese rescuers clawed bare-handed at the rubble. It was a ghastly scene. The bodies of four Vietnamese staffers were laid out together, awaiting the ambulances. Even then, I wondered how I could feel so detached, but in this kind of situation my journalistic role was that of witness, emotions kept buried. It was different when we entered part of the main building that remained intact. Our intent was merely to get a high-angle shot of the wreckage and confusion below, but there in a second-floor room we found the French Head of Mission.

He had been laid on a table beneath a whirling ceiling fan, naked except for some cotton cloth covering his groin. He was still alive, but mercifully unconscious, his body a horror of third-degree burns. Fujii looked at me but I shook my head. This we didn't need to film, *shouldn't* film — in that much I could help.

Of course, I cabled CTV describing what we had witnessed and filmed, and Tom Gould cabled back: "Your eyewitnesser carried internationally by AP. Created great excitement in U.S. Good job. Have contract with CBS." Then a second cable: "Can you call CTV newsroom soonest with voicer for tonight's news."

Ah, if only I could find a phone!

A third cable stressed the urgent need for the film in "view Laird contention could be exploding SAM missile not U.S. bomb." Secretary of Defense Melvin Laird, who two years earlier after our filming of a POW prison had emphatically called it a "show camp," now conjured another whopper: the U.S., he told the press, had been targeting a railroad centre some three miles away and he suggested that a faulty anti-aircraft missile fired at the Phantom jets had "fallen back on the city."

But this time the U.S. media were buying none of it. With the time difference, on the same day as the event all the main evening newscasts were quoting the AP wire that "Canadian television reporter Michael Maclear says he saw three jets swoop over the heart of the capital, with no possibility of pilot error." Using my byline, the *New York Times* headlined "Witness Describes Attack by U.S. Jets." The next day a French cryptographer at the consulate described feeling the impact of "two explosions" with no evidence of some stray SAM. And the death toll had risen to seven, with French anger mounting. In response to Laird, I had cabled that French Mission officials had found "fragments of bombs" amid the debris. And probing even more, the *San Francisco Examiner* reported that permission to escalate the bombing was the "result of a top secret order approved by the Joint Chiefs of Staff."

Even then, and for the next ten days, the Pentagon kept misleading the public. On October 21 the *Times* quoted Laird deputy Jerry W. Friedheim as conceding that the bombing of Hanoi had happened but still insisted it was an accident, offering a convoluted explanation that the bombing had "probably resulted from a mechanical failure in a bomb release system in which a 500-pound bomb did not fall until after the plane carrying it had pulled out of the bombing dive." As quoted by the *Times*, Friedheim then stated that at the time two dozen Navy F-4 and A-7 jets from the carrier Midway were "attacking a railway yard and transhipment point about three miles northeast" of the French mission. In fact, the Pentagon had now knowingly revealed that the off-limits bombing of Hanoi and its sister port city of Haiphong was no longer in force.

This merely fuelled international disbelief and concern. What might occur next? No one doubted that the bombing of the consulate had been a tragic error, but the Pentagon excuse of the pilots not knowing they were over central Hanoi was patently absurd.

At the same time, the Head of Mission Pierre Susine — flown to Paris — died from his horrific wounds and French public and media outrage shook the government. Without directly blaming France's close ally, President Pompidou personally called the outcome "deplorable" and this obliged the U.S. Secretary of State William Rogers to express "deep concern" and to promise a full "investigation" — in diplomatic parlance, an admission of guilt in all but words.

But the concern the world media began to voice was whether the unprecedented sortie of F-4 Phantoms over the heart of Hanoi had been no error, with some token bombing intended. At this time, President Richard Nixon was seeking re-election on a platform of total withdrawal from Vietnam, but in Paris at the time of the bombing, chief negotiator Henry Kissinger had just spent a frustrating week in private talks with Hanoi's Politburo negotiator, Le Duc Tho. Kissinger's pitch was being described in the U.S. media as "deal with me" or "there's no knowing" what Nixon might do.

Increasingly, it seemed that the first-ever bombing of Hanoi was an intended warning. Our camera, a mile from the scene, had not captured the few seconds flyover, but our filming of the carnage at the French consulate was graphic; if this was what just two bombs could do then Hanoi had to be fearing the destructive might of B-52s unleashed on the city. Perhaps to comfort the populace, it was announced that the legendary General Vo Nguyen Giap, now Minister of Defence, would henceforth personally conduct Hanoi's aerial defence.

The tea leaves were telling me that after almost thirty years of needless Great Power war the Vietnam saga might be nearing its end, but with the worst still to come.

I was told Prime Minister Pham Van Dong had agreed to be interviewed on the overall situation, but there was no fixed date. I could but wait, each day watching the hotel rooftop rehearsals of my guerrilla-waitress with ever greater respect and trepidation. CTV wanted me back for a special half hour once I had Pham's assessment of events, and in the meantime cabled me, saying "Heard from Dan Rather CBS used four minutes of quote your excellent Hanoi perspective."

This was the kind of morale booster I wasn't used to! The cable was signed by Don Cameron, who at the time I left CBC was producing *Newsmagazine*. Cameron had become the latest key defector to join CTV as Tom Gould's deputy. I briefly wondered how my old network had handled the bombing of the French consulate and the early denial of spin-specialist Melvin Laird, whom they had seemingly believed in the earlier POW controversy. But in truth it was rare now that I ever thought of the Network — and it would remain thus for many decades.

* * *

In the days after our filming of the October 11th bombing, I would find Hanoi officials unusually confiding. Clearly, whether influenced by the bombing or not, the peace talks had advanced, yet this mere factor — the expectations — added to the fear of unknown consequences should the talks again collapse.

On October 23, 1972, an analysis I had sent to the *New York Times* — front-paged — began: "The highest authorities here believe that a settlement of the Vietnam War is more possible than not, but there is no conviction that agreement is definite. Much of the detail of a settlement has been 'orally reached' and problems were only 'between Washington and Saigon.' Hanoi cannot understand that the United States feels it difficult to dictate peace terms to Saigon.

"At the highest level here, the peace negotiations are still described as possibly pre-election acrobatics."

The sense of a heightened effort at a peace deal grew with the arrival in Hanoi for *Newsweek* of eminent American journalist Arnaud de Borchgrave, who was close to Kissinger. Over Tiger beer at the hotel, de Borchgrave confided he had just come from a lengthy interview with Pham Van Dong, whose French he described as "perfection." And the prime minister was apparently confirming a potential deal.

My interview with Pham, a day after that of de Borchgrave, would reflect how hugely crucial decisions could shift in the space of twenty-four hours.

In the interim, Pham had learned that the U.S. had again failed to get the acceptance of Saigon's President Nguyen Van Thieu to the otherwise agreed peace terms. Washington was asking for more time to persuade Thieu, but Pham, in my interview with him, when asked if a peace agreement was close, would only say that he hoped so but there was "no certainty."

Then, off-camera, unburdening his doubts, he said he could not promise peace. Nothing was firm, Nixon was not to be trusted, and the time Nixon wanted was merely to get past election day.

* * *

A few hours later, an aide of the prime minister came to the hotel as I was packing for the ICC flight to Vientiane that evening. He had a "very urgent" message: the PM had spoken "too candidly," he was concerned of the consequences, and would I please not quote his comments regarding Nixon. So I did not.

But once more at Vientiane airport I called the *New York Times* and CTV, citing a "highly placed source as having serious doubts as to any imminent peace agreement."

It made the *Times* front-page newsflash column on November 6 at the same time as a *Newsweek* election-day cover trumpeting "Peace Is at Hand."

In a special CTV program, I quoted unidentified sources as saying it came down to this: on the signing of a peace treaty, the U.S. wanted the immediate release of all POWs and the North wanted agreement that its troops in the South, then estimated at 150,000, would remain in place until Hanoi and Saigon reached agreement on some form of a coalition. These were essentially the same terms as those negotiated some four years earlier just prior to the death of Ho Chi Minh. But again Washington could not get Saigon's acceptance.

It meant total deadlock — and the war's most dangerous phase with a re-elected President Nixon (with 60.7 percent of the popular vote) mandated to end the war, but with few U.S. troops remaining in Vietnam and with the Saigon government demonstrably incapable of defending itself.

A year earlier, in a test of self-reliance, the southern army, ARVN, had suffered huge 50 percent casualties in an all-out attempt to seize and hold the Ho Chi Minh Trail at its most vulnerable point just below the DMZ partition line. In fairness, it was an undertaking the U.S. military had more than once considered and rejected as certain to mean unacceptable casualties. In retaliation, some ten NV infantry and mechanized divisions swept across the DMZ in a brief invasion which convinced Hanoi how easy the endgame could be.

In early December 1972 Hanoi's entire delegation walked out of the Paris peace talks, vowing not to return. But secret communications continued. Kissinger, on Nixon's orders, now reportedly informed his counterpart Le Duc Tho that a complete breakdown of negotiations would result in the use of massive force against the North. In parallel, Saigon's President Thieu was warned that U.S. military aid would cease totally if he did not accept the proposed settlement. But both South and North remained defiant. Thieu simply didn't believe the world's foremost superpower could afford the indignity of just walking away — and in that much he was to be proved right.

As for Hanoi, though the settlement meant recognizing the Saigon regime, the Northern troops would remain in place in the South until a coalition was worked out, if ever. For Hanoi, come what may, eventual reunification on its terms now seemed in sight.

For Nixon, starting his second term, another four years of war seemed all too probable. So began the horrific end. On December 18, despite Henry Kissinger's reported opposition, the United States began the most intensive urban bombing in the history of warfare.

All at once, no fewer than 120 giant B-52s struck Hanoi and its twin port city Haiphong with unrelenting fury. The bombing would last for eleven days and nights until December 30, with a halt on Christmas Day, a battle known to protesting world media as the "Twelve Days of Christmas."

But Hanoi's defense team, led by General Vo Nguyen Giap, noticed that the bombers, coming from bases in the Philippines and Thailand, kept to the same flight pattern.

On the third day, Hanoi claimed its SAM missiles had brought down six of the bombers and that by the fourth day forty-three American pilots had been killed or captured — and several on being shown the destruction paraded before cameras expressing regrets. In the recorded words of one of them filmed by Denpa News, "To my extreme surprise I could observe no military targets...."

Though most of the U.S. media condemned the bombing, the *New York Times* stating "Civilized man will be horrified" and the *Los Angeles Times* calling it "beyond all reason," for Nixon there could be no backing off. As revealed in my book *Vietnam: The Ten Thousand Day War*, Kissinger aide Winston Lord explained the Nixon administration reasoning for the mass bombing of Hanoi: "The President had to demonstrate we couldn't be trifled with — and, frankly, demonstrate our toughness to Thieu."

Earlier, at the very time I witnessed the first ever bombing of Hanoi, October 1972, Winston Lord was accompanying Kissinger for protracted bargaining in Saigon with Nguyen Van Thieu ("He Who Ascends"), then president for the past five years. There they presented Thieu with a peace agreement accepted by both the U.S. and North Vietnam, requiring only Thieu's acceptance and to be ceremonially signed by all parties on October 31st — a date so close to the initial October 11 bombing of Hanoi that now, in piecing together these dates and secret talks, the October 11 attack was a pre-planned warning to both North and South to collaborate — and accelerate — U.S. military withdrawal from Vietnam. As Winston Lord told us, the U.S. promised continuance of military aid to the South and the North had accepted this, but Thieu "blasted the agreement," which would allow Northern troops to remain in place in the South. As Thieu himself told us, "I am not a yes-man. I am not a puppet. I acted as a patriot, and as a president who is responsible for the fate of our country."

"We miscalculated," said Winston Lord, but with Nixon's re-election in November the December "Christmas" bombing became his choice for bringing to heel both North and South Vietnam.

In the final days, the U.S. military estimated that Hanoi had expended a thousand SAM missiles; some one hundred thousand bombs had been dropped on two small adjoining cities. By then, at least sixty American pilots and aircrew were reported killed or captured. The end seemed to come from the sheer exhaustion of both sides. But the peace terms remained unchanged, only now Saigon's President Thieu got a take-it-or-leave it pledge that the U.S. would guarantee the safety of the South (which Nixon might have done but for Watergate and his consequent impeachment).

During the bombing, I tried in vain to contact my Japanese colleagues, imagining their nights in the Thong Nhat's makeshift air raid shelter where earlier Joan Baez sang a lament and Jane Fonda bravely spoke her mind. Sadly, I would not see Fujii again.

On January 27, 1973, all sides signed a peace treaty in Paris. The two chief negotiators, Kissinger and Le Duc Tho, were subsequently awarded the Nobel Peace Prize — which only Kissinger accepted. With exceptional candour, John Negroponte, one of the U.S. peace team, later told us, "The peace treaty did nothing for Saigon. We got our prisoners back; we were able to end our direct military involvement. But there were no ostensible benefits for Saigon to justify all of the enormous effort and bloodshed of the previous years."

Hanoi called the settlement "A decisive victory, an aerial equivalent to Dien Bien Phu."

On March 28, 1973, after eight years of combat and twenty years of military involvement, the last American servicemen in Saigon boarded a flight for home, nine thousand miles away. In those two lost decades, almost six million GIs had rotated through 'Nam, and on the official Washington memorial the embossed names of American military who died in Vietnam would total 58,195.

Vietnamese casualties were some forty times as great! At least one million Vietnamese soldiers from both South and North died, as well as that many civilians on both sides, mostly during the combat.

For as many decades as the war had lasted, the pain would remain.

CHAPTER THIRTEEN
The War Comes Home

FOR ME, AT THIS time, there was no inner peace over my reportage from Vietnam. In three extended wartime visits to the North I believed I had reported accurately. But with the White House disputing — and my network seemingly disowning me — a mental wound remained. A year after Vietnam's shaky peace, now permanently back in Canada with a weekly series underway for CTV, a priority for me was getting the facts on the controversial Christmas Day filming of the POW prison that had been debunked by Washington as a "show camp."

What followed was an insight on a torn nation and a bitterness that would still divide Americans as they went to the polls thirty-five years later.

With the peace treaty signed, Hanoi had provided an updated list of 555 POW names, increasing to 661 from all war regions, with fifty-five American prisoners having died during the seven-and-a-half-year period of captivity. All would be returned stateside, and, after medical treatment and military debriefings, released within a few weeks into a society in no mood for national hurrahs. Unlike World War Two and Korea, in which America was the saviour, wars in which the good and bad guys were undisputed, the Vietnam veterans returned to a nation divided as never before, with the trauma of the veterans largely unrealized and unattended.

At CTV, with the freedom to choose the subjects of my weekly documentary series, we produced several early post-war profiles of the cold-shoulder homecoming. We extensively filmed veteran self-help groups trying to forget and to adapt after a war that had brutalized the military. We told the story of the CIA's secret war of abduction of supposed Viet Cong sympathizers — a torture-and-kill operation about which

CIA Director William Colby later testified before Congress that tens of thousands had died, without trial and without proof of the charges. We filmed the conditions varying from grim to outrageous in the hospitals and care centres for Vietnam veterans which the seriously wounded had endured for years, their physical and mental state a national disgrace.

Our research up to the late seventies revealed 120,000 suicides of American veterans. One third of the U.S. combat force in Vietnam had become drug-addicted, and some 500,000 veterans received "other than honourable" discharge. Essentially, as the war dragged on with no clear purpose, it increasingly morally numbed combat GIs, many of whom turned to crime once back home.

One young veteran I interviewed on camera in the compound of a California prison was serving life for a contract killing he undertook for just a few dollars. Perhaps an extreme case, perhaps not, but in a much-needed unburdening he told how 'Nam brutalized him, how he shot down a pregnant young woman during a village patrol.

"I fired a burst of about five or six at her. She hit the ground and rolled over and I knew it was a girl then, and it flashed through my mind all the complications I'd have going over there if she's still alive, so I just went ahead and killed her.

"She was about eighteen or nineteen, I guess. She was pregnant. I don't know why she darted out of the doorway like that. Her mom came running out, screaming, and somebody killed her mom. And after that, you know, I didn't have to kill that girl. It was easier to kill her than it was to go help her.

"If we came across civilians, burn their house, take what you wanted, mess with their women, stuff like that. Mutilating bodies, collecting ears and heads, doing sexual acts on dead bodies, torturing people, stuff like that."

And before he went to Vietnam? "I couldn't conceive of America being wrong."

Such was the fate of so many of the boys, sent to win hearts and minds, who lost their own.

America's turning away from the plight of the veterans was, to my mind, on par with — and a consequence of — its blindness as to the nationalist nature of North Vietnam and thus the protracted war it portended, which successive occupants of the White House preferred not to recognize, always assuring Americans "The boys will be home for Christmas."

The price that American GIs paid was for me as important to record as the price the North Vietnamese paid. And in comparison to the U.S. combat force in South Vietnam, the pilots held prisoner in the North as a whole suffered nothing of consequence. Their homecoming was relatively easy, except for those pilots who, while in captivity, had opposed the war.

Those POWs were not like the young conscripts thrown into a war of attrition in the South. Most of the POWs were high-ranking career officers who never faced the "enemy" until made captive, but who despite their rank were not supposed, or allowed to think for themselves. So the second thoughts of some of them, as told on national television, seemingly troubled the White House far more than the day-to-day horrors in the South — troubled it enough to knowingly lie to the American public.

With the release of the POWs, our researchers set about tracing the two pilots I'd interviewed in captivity some two years earlier. One of them, Navy Commander Robert Schweitzer, was reported in the U.S. media to have died in "an auto accident" soon after his return home, and then said to have been "buried at sea."

The other interviewee, Navy Captain Walter Eugene Wilber, together with U.S.A.F. Lieutenant Colonel Edison Miller, one of the seven POWs filmed in the prison exercise yard, agreed to be re-interviewed in Toronto. I had no idea what they would say — we didn't ask them. We wanted spontaneity. Whatever they had to say, we wanted the viewers to hear it first.

When filming the POWs in 1970 I had no knowledge whatsoever of their background. Until entering the prison I didn't even know their names. Likewise, in connecting with Wilber and Miller in the United States, we knew only that they had been honourably discharged and awarded the Distinguished Flying Cross for valour.

The U.S. military revealed only that Wilber had been the senior officer in his squadron, had been cited for bravery in the Korean War, was married, now with four sons and a daughter, and had been shot down in his F-4 Phantom on his twentieth mission on Father's Day, June 16, 1968.

Miller, also a veteran of the Korean War, was the perfect poster soldier, a teenage enlistee who had made it from private to colonel. He was squadron commander on his seventieth mission when his two-man F-4B Phantom was shot down by an AA barrage October 13, 1967, the co-pilot killed. Miller's parachute ripped and he had a hard landing, suffering several crushed vertebra and a broken ankle. He reported that he was force-marched for forty days to initial captivity in Hanoi's Hoa Lo French-era prison — which the American captives would sardonically nickname the Hanoi Hilton. In total, Wilber would be a prisoner for four and a half years, Miller for almost five and a half years.

Yet for them both the far longer drama would be the homecoming. Not least how to treat them would set the military brass against each other in courtroom after courtroom verdict worthy of a You Be the Judge movie.

Much later it became known that in 1971, soon after the Christmas Day interviews, the U.S. Department of Defense set up a "Prisoner of War Policy Committee," its chair no less than Secretary of Defense Melvin Laird, who'd ridiculed our filming as "a staged production."

After "intense" deliberation it ruled that on the eventual so-called "Operation Homecoming" there would be "no propaganda statement prosecutions" and that "no charges could be brought against any POW — except by another POW."

Those last four words would prove classic bureaucratic double-speak, negating the committee's main objective of letting sleeping dogs lie.

Nothing about the committee was known then to the media or to the American public, a secrecy influenced by the heightening anti-war demonstrations of that time, including violent protests outside the Pentagon, so on the one hand the ruling, if known, might seem to be appeasing the anti-war movement, and on the other hand might be seen as setting the POWs against each other, potentially inflaming national division.

But with the peace settlement and America's final troop withdrawal two years later, and with the first POWs released on February 12, 1973, public passions had largely cooled. And to keep it that way the process of POW debriefings was tightly controlled, so the accusations by some POWs against other POWs went unknown outside the high command.

In this cloaked "Operation Homecoming" a total of thirteen U.S. servicemen were charged with various misconduct, with the most numerous charges levelled against Navy Captain Wilber and Marine Corps

Lieutenant Colonel Miller — brought by the highest-ranking POW, Rear Admiral James B. Stockdale, held prisoner for seven and a half years at the Hoa Lo prison in downtown Hanoi.

The Hoa Lo was where the highest-profile Americans were kept, including (later Senator) Captain John McCain, whose father and grandfather had been Admirals of the Fleet. Miller would also be imprisoned at the Hoa Lo for years before being transferred to the prison where Wilber was held — the prison where we filmed them both.

Now, back home, the charges against them included making propaganda statements, coercing and informing on fellow prisoners, accepting favours from the enemy, and refusing to obey the orders of the senior POW, namely Stockdale.

Under the "Operation Homecoming" guidelines, such charges by a fellow POW did not mean a court-martial, nor did the charges have the automatic endorsement of the Navy or the U.S. Department of Defense — even though, collectively, the charges amounted to mutiny. Rather, it had been pre-agreed that such charges would be referred up the line for consideration by a specially appointed military board. Initially, the decision in the Wilber-Miller case was swift. Both men had denied all charges, stating that any of their actions were ones of conscience.

Without directly addressing each charge, the Judge Advocate for the Navy, himself a rear admiral but acting for the overall armed forces, pointed out that some charges — such as propaganda statements by POWs — had already officially been exempt from prosecution by the military, and other charges were non-specific.

As later revealed, the Judge Advocate noted that any trial might be prolonged and "accompanied by great publicity" with the likelihood of conviction "marginal." In other words, charges hard to prove might rekindle and enlarge the public debate on the morality of America's undeclared war.

On July 3, 1973, just six months after the homecoming, the Secretary of the Navy dismissed the charges but issued a letter of censure to be part of the service records of both Wilber and Miller, stating their conduct at times was detrimental to the morale of other prisoners. Both men, freed from any charges, retired from service with full benefits, with Miller receiving a promotion entitlement to full colonel.

But Miller, acting on another entitlement, immediately appealed to have the letter of censure expunged. This the Navy high command resisted. Now military lawyers began taking sides. A long nightmare began.

In our discussions in Toronto, Wilber and Miller revealed none of this, nor could they with their secretive case now under appeal and in its preposterous third year of deliberation by the Board of Correction of Naval Records (BCNR). None of this had reached the public. And had it done so it would be inconceivable that the case would drag on into the next two decades. In that much, the case epitomized America's twenty-year unresolved, no-win involvement in Vietnam, and America's prolonged post-war inability to put the war behind it.

At CTV, preparing to re-interview the POWs, we had our own wry situation. We planned to run clips from the 1970 Christmas Day interview so as to remind both viewers and the two pilots what was said. But the film was with CBC Archives, which wanted U.S. $90 per second of film used, so that our intended clips, running perhaps four minutes, would have cost $18,000 — the bulk of our budget. "It's very historic footage," said the lady archivist I spoke to, and she wouldn't budge. It hurt!

The exclusive film the Network had been so doubtful about at the time was now "historic." An event that had been so costly for me was now to cost more. A friendly "No charge — you're welcome" would have been appropriate. Instead we agreed on U.S. $90 a second *used*.

On getting the film reel, we selected a few frames totalling less than a second, enlarged them to five by five-foot posters and sent CBC a cheque for U.S. $90. That felt good!

In the studio, Wilber and Miller sat in front of the enlarged prison scenes. We had filmed Wilber in a room inside the prison, Miller outside among the exercise group. At this stage, I still knew nothing much about them. In a get-to-know you conversation, Wilber spoke adoringly of his five children and his wife, Jeannie, a music teacher in Millerton, Pennsylvania, saying her strength and their Methodist faith had enabled his survival.

Miller, though married, revealed little of his private life; a defiant maverick, his car license plate read "POW"! Clearly, both men had no fear of questioning and were receiving only their travel expenses, so now their only incentive was in what they wanted to say.

Would their story now change?

In a very real way, the tension for me was as great as at the time of the interview in the prison camp. I had found some comfort in telling myself that even if the actions of the White House and the Pentagon proved justified, which I considered highly unlikely, the manner in which my own network had displayed doubt and disloyalty was certainly wrong — not least, a disservice to its public. So now, admittedly, I was hoping for vindication.

As a reminder for viewers and for Wilber and Miller, we first ran Secretary of Defense Melvin Laird's "show camp" description. "It was certainly very carefully controlled, a staged as well as censored production," he told a special press conference — wording that might be construed as saying that I was a party to what he alleged. So, my first question: "Was the place we filmed an actual prison camp?"

"Yes," Miller said instantly, and Wilber added, "That was a prison camp since 1965, except for a nine-month period there were American prisoners at that camp all the time." And the Pentagon with its round-the-clock satellites must have known this.

Wilber: "That building was our building. No more than three to a room and identical rooms."

I told them I thought at the time the twinkling Christmas tree seemed staged, but Miller said they had a Christmas tree every year and "We were given a Christmas meal in our tradition every Christmas I was there."

Were some of them better treated on condition they talked? Wilber: "We were not under any duress or coercion. We had the opportunity to say yes or no as we wished."

Miller: "It helped the American people to know we were alive and well-treated."

Wilber: "We felt it an excellent way of letting people back home know; a little information is better than none."

Miller: "We were told President Nixon made statements that the prisoners in Vietnam were the worst treated of the century, so I believe that President Nixon used the prisoners and prisoner issues for his own propaganda."

What about the stories of torture after the POWs returned home?

Miller: "Some of my debriefing officers, when I described some of the forms of punishment I went through, in their opinion it was torture. I didn't think so. Many times I was caught for various infractions of prison rules — trying to communicate with other Americans, refusing to bow, things like that, and I would be hit with a rifle butt, pushed around, forced to bow, but to me that's any prison environment."

Were the majority of prisoners tortured, or not?

Miller: "Well, it's a matter of definition, but I don't believe so."

How, as servicemen in uniform, did they become anti-war?

Wilber: "I went to Vietnam with a question as to why we hadn't declared war on this country. It became an agony for me because my conscience told me there was no legal justification for the war."

Miller: "Although I had doubts as to the legality, morality of the war, I dismissed them with the fact Congress was giving the money to sustain this war and I was a professional soldier, not a politician."

Wilber: "We are all guilty of loyalty to our immediate boss, to let it overtake and overcome every personal feeling we had."

Miller: "We had to go to the very core of our being — loyalty, what is it, where does it belong?"

Wilber: "It would have to be to a very high principle. It has to be beyond institution. It would have to be to a principle which caused the institution to be made in the first place."

How perfectly said! So often institutions that should guide us forget or abandon their founding principles.

So it would prove for Wilber and Miller as government institutions fudged for years over whether or not to censure them — a trial of a kind that had the all-too-familiar smell of dysfunctional management bent on imposing authority.

It would be an astounding seven years before the Navy rendered a verdict on the appeal against censure, with the Board for Correction of Naval Records recommending that the censure be removed. It would be another three years, 1982, before the Navy high command reviewed the recommendation — and rejected it!

A defiant Miller then sued the Secretary of the Navy in the U.S. Court of Appeals, District of Columbia, which based its lengthy review on whether there was sufficient and specific evidence of the charges that had resulted in censure.

At this stage, almost a decade after the U.S. had withdrawn from Vietnam, the strange and disparate world of the POW camps came to be known. In total in North Vietnam there were thirteen POW camps, five of them located in Hanoi or its adjoining suburbs. Only one of them had an official name: the Hoa Lo, its name from the French era, a huge grim fortress of a prison where the Viet Minh who opposed French colonialism were kept in barbaric conditions, so that the mere mention of Hoa Lo conjured visions of constant degradation and torture. For sure, its ambiance alone must have felt torturous, but on the other hand its central Hanoi location for most of the war made it the safest prison from air strikes.

Eventually, to the U.S. media and moviegoers — but not to the POWs as a whole — the Hoa Lo was better known as the Hanoi Hilton. In fact, the captives in all the Hanoi-area POW prisons at times used "Hanoi Hilton" as a mock label for camps that had no official name.

Years later, at a national POW "recognition day" assembly, Edison Miller spoke of spending years at the "Hanoi Hilton," meaning the Hoa Lo, while at the same event Wilber said he had spent "fifty-six months at the Hanoi Hilton" — that is, at the camp where I filmed him.

On arriving there, with the blindfolds removed, the first thing I asked my minders was the name of the camp. "No name," I was told. Like the bombed southern provinces I had earlier visited, militarily sensitive places such as evacuated factories were known only by given numbers. So it was with the prison camps, and so the POWs devised cynical nicknames that became known after the war. In Hanoi, in addition to the officially named Hao Lo, the other camps got sad-joke names like Funny Farm, Country Club, Camp Faith, Zoo, and Plantation.

Plantation would fit what we partly filmed. We saw its wide gardens, its pretty pond with overhanging willow trees, its laced bamboo entrance to a single storey-brick building where Wilber and Miller said the prison rooms were all alike. Despite the high prison walls and mounted guard towers, Plantation would have been a descriptive name for much of what we saw. Quite likely its alternate inmate choice of name — Zoo — was intended to capture the not-so-pretty POW existence the visitor didn't get to see. In all the camps, prisoners were kept segregated in small groups, and perhaps conditions varied. But the issue for me was whether we had been "duped" in what we did see, whether this was a "show camp" — meaning that prisoners were never kept there, and thus whether or not Wilber and Miller and others were accurate and sincere in what they had to say.

In the "Plantation" prison camp, Wilber and Miller were part of a small anti-war group which decided it was not subject to the authority of the senior POW at the Hoa Lo, with Miller himself being the most senior captive Marine. They reasoned that since this was an undeclared war they were not prisoners of war but "Americans detained by a foreign power." This was not a stance the U.S. courts were likely to entertain, nor did they, yet Miller in particular persisted year after year with what amounted to an appeal for the same freedom of opinion on the war granted to any American. What did influence the U.S. Court of Appeals was the lack of precise evidence on many of the charges; in effect, the total lack of communication between the different prisons, and the segregation of prisoners within them, which made the charges against Miller and others almost impossible to prove.

In 1985, twelve years after the POW homecoming, the Columbia District Court of Appeals gave its verdict. It ordered the censure removed — the second court to do so. But the Columbia Appeals Court also ordered the Board for Correction of Navy Records, which had been first to absolve Wilber and Miller, to review its earlier decision, presumably to demonstrate overall agreement that the censure be removed.

Another three years would pass before the final verdict. Precisely what — or who — influenced the puzzling outcome remains undocumented. On May 17, 1988, the BCNR reversed itself, deciding that censure was warranted, and so it remains on the military records of Miller, Wilber, and others.

The case had been before the courts for over fifteen years, nearly twice the length of time the U.S. was in combat in Vietnam! And the case was not over yet: legally over, but recurring again and again to add heat — and bitterness — to national elections.

The most senior POW, Rear Admiral James B. Stockdale, who had brought the charges against Miller and others and whose accusations had prevailed within the military high command, now emerged as a major political figure. And perhaps explaining his influence, James Bond Stockdale would subsequently claim to have personal knowledge of huge historical importance, information that led to U.S. combat.

At the homecoming, Stockdale stood out not least due to his injuries and his citations. He had been one of the longest held POWs, a prisoner for seven and a half years at the grim Hoa Lo, much of the time in solitary confinement and "routinely tortured," according to one biography. Though physically handicapped on returning home (a Californian, like Miller) he stayed in the Navy, getting a series of promotions, ultimately becoming a rear admiral and receiving the Medal of Honor to cap his twenty-six decorations.

Stockdale served as President of the Naval War College during the late seventies and from 1981–88, the years when military and civilian courts wrestled over the fate of Colonel Edison Miller, Stockdale was Chair of the White House Fellows — a kind of Reagan-chosen posse of patriots. Then, in election year 1992, the maverick Texan multi-millionaire Ross Perot ran for the presidency as an independent, with Stockdale as his nominal vice president, against incumbent President George H. Bush and Arkansas Governor William Jefferson Clinton.

Stockdale's first public political speech proved something of a fumbling classic as he began it by asking "Who am I? Why am I here?" Anticipating soul-searching insight on Vietnam and Iraq, his audience eagerly applauded those opening words. But then what followed seemed so rambling and unconnected that he was mocked on *Saturday Night Live*.

Later, as quoted in a biography in Wikipedia, Stockdale blamed the difficulty of conveying his long suffering as a POW, and his sense of himself as having "started" the American bombing of North Vietnam. In a filmed campaign speech, he suddenly blurted out, "I know things about the Vietnam War better than anybody in the world, I know how governments, American government, can be...." — then he paused, seemingly stunned, and said no more, though he would in later years.

The bombing which President Lyndon Johnson ordered, and which, unknown to the American media and public, grew to mass bombing of civilian regions, began in August 1964, followed by deployment of American combat troops in South Vietnam in March 1965, all authorized by Congress in the belief that North Vietnamese torpedo boats had twice directly attacked the U.S. destroyer *Maddox* in international waters.

The attack supposedly occurred in the Gulf of Tonkin, the main supply lifeline for Hanoi and the port of Haiphong, waters where President Johnson had considered laying mines, but feared the risk of destroying Soviet or Chinese cargo ships, which could trigger a far wider conflict.

Much later, official investigation of the "Tonkin Gulf affair" found that there had been an initial skirmish but no direct attacks on the *Maddox*.

Before getting Congressional approval for the intensified war, the U.S. response to the first supposed "attack" was air strikes by jet fighter aircraft based on the offshore carrier *Ticonderoga*. Four F-8 Crusader jets wiped out Hanoi-area fuel depots.

On that first major air attack on the North the squadron leader was Commander James Bond Stockdale. Then, on August 4, 1964, the date of the reported North Vietnamese torpedo attacks, Stockdale was on reconnaissance flight duty. Decades later, in remarks attributed to him in Wikipedia, he told of having "the best seat in the house" that August 4th while flying over the Gulf of Tonkin: "Our destroyers were shooting at phantom targets — there were no PT boats there, there was nothing there but black water and American firepower." He is further quoted as saying he was ordered to keep silent.

A year after the Gulf of Tonkin rationale for all-out war, Stockdale was flying a Skyhawk on the now-daily air attacks on the North when shot down September 9, 1965, beginning more than seven years imprisonment at the Hoa Lo, where his interrogators would certainly have learned of his role in the initial bombing.

There, by his own account in solitary confinement much of the time, he would have no means of contact with POWs at other camps. Any charges against any of them would thus be third-hand at best. But this aside — and if accepting the statements of Stockdale as quoted — the crucial question is: Who was the greater offender, Edison W. Miller, who while in uniform spoke out against the war, or James B. Stockdale, who, while in uniform, hid the truth he says he witnessed — the one event used to justify massive escalation of the war — and then for decades kept silent, even as he sought the office of vice president?

What was loyalty; where did it lie? Obeying orders you knew were wrong was highly dubious loyalty.

The Perot-Stockdale independent ticket got an impressive 20 percent of the popular vote; just possibly it might have got far more votes if it had laid out all the facts, if it had encouraged healing national debate on the Vietnam War.

Instead, POW politics lived on, fed by the division over new wars in Iraq and Afghanistan. In the 2008 presidential election the campaign strategists for Republican candidate Senator John McCain seemed to needlessly play up his Vietnam War record, perhaps because the Democrat candidate Barack Obama hadn't been in any war.

Now, thirty-five years after war's end, an indirect spat between McCain and Miller, both survivors of Hoa Lo who never met there face-to-face, seemed representative of a still-divided nation. McCain became captive in October 1967, one month after Miller, when his navy Skyhawk was shot down on a raid slightly north of Hanoi, but with his parachute drifting into the city lake, where he might have drowned. Pulled out, he instantly became the most prized of the POW pawns because of his lineage: son of Admiral John S. "Jack" McCain Jr., one-time commander-in-chief of all U.S. Pacific forces. According to unofficial accounts, McCain received hospital treatment for his substantial injuries. According to the official U.S. Navy account McCain was "crippled from serious and ill-treated injuries" and "steadfastly refused offers of (early) freedom."

The official record states that McCain's resistance resulted in "extreme mental and physical cruelties." For this, he was later awarded the Silver Star Medal, for a total of seventeen medals and citations.

Long after the 1988 final decision in the Miller case, McCain, now a senator and previously the Navy's liaison to the U.S. Senate during the final drawn-out years of the Miller trial, would reopen the issue of the rebellious POWs in his 1999 book *Faith of My Fathers*, a bestseller right up to McCain's 2008 bid for the presidency.

In the book, relating his years in captivity, McCain without naming his targets writes about "two camp rats" who "lost faith completely" — the two being subsequently identified as Miller and Wilber in a June 15, 2008 *New York Times* article on presidential candidate McCain's war views. As quoted, McCain's accusations described the unnamed POWs as "collaborators, actively aiding the enemy," a description which the earlier exhaustive court hearings did not use, and contrasting sharply with the letter of censure against Miller and Wilber which stated "Your conduct was severely detrimental to the welfare and morale of fellow prisoners."

The *Times* article arose from an "essay" McCain wrote in 1974, a year after the homecoming, for the National War College, supposedly to be kept confidential but which suddenly surfaced in the 2008 election year and which, not least, regarded later captives as "exposed to the divisive forces ... of the anti-war movement in the United States."

So now, thirty-five years since the "peace," long-dormant passions and divisions became election fodder, bringing scalding counterattacks by Miller on McCain's own prison record.

As to his own POW record, Miller acknowledged that "I did stand up and say the war was wrong. I would speak out against the war, but I never spoke against my country. And I gave up no secrets."

At the time in question, Miller as well as Wilber was imprisoned at the Plantation, so McCain at the Hoa Lo could have had no direct knowledge of the POWs elsewhere. But possibly McCain heard a loudspeaker voicing of an anti-war tape which Miller and Wilber admitted making.

Miller, after leaving the Navy, became divorced but like Wilber he had a large family: seven sons and a daughter. For a time, he served as supervisor of Orange County, California, then began a new career as a criminal defense lawyer, remaining in his eighties an active member of the California Bar.

After my repeat interview with Wilber and Miller, I had no further contact with them. But it seems to me, given their long service in the military, including the Korean War, and in Miller's case his unyielding fifteen-year fight against censure, that their anti-war statements on Vietnam were — as they claimed — a matter of conscience.

After all, regarding Vietnam, it was many years before the public anti-war movement took hold in the United States, so couldn't the same misgivings have belatedly troubled and motivated a percentage of those in uniform?

Loyalty, where does it lie? is a continuing question for any — and every — kind of institution.

American POWs playing basketball in what the Pentagon called a "show camp."

Colonel Edison Miller in the exercise yard with a book titled *The Unheard Voices*.

Navy commander Walter E. Wilbur, a POW who turned anti-war.

Bombing victims.
"This war must stop,
stop now," said Wilbur.

The author and Prime Minister Pham Van Dong before the Christmas Day 1970 filming of POWs.

The author at Hoa Lo, the French-era prison. (Photo by Michael Ellis.)

CHAPTER FOURTEEN
History Calling

LOOKING BACK, IT IS astonishing to realize that when I next went to Hanoi in 1979, to commence the first television history of the war, Miller was still awaiting a hearing, and when I returned there again two decades later, in 2003, Miller and his critics would be at each other's throats through the presidential election years that followed. In all that time, the American people had been largely subject to recrimination rather than rational debate on their then longest-ever war.

Defense lawyer Miller fought for fifteen years in the courts for a personal hearing that was never granted; America was involved even longer in a war few Americans truly understood — a war in which the U.S. military had no precise plan, nor date, for an ending. Even with the U.S. withdrawal, Americans could not be certain their war was over. President Nixon had pledged to defend the South in the event the North attacked. But then, on August 9, 1974, Nixon — facing impeachment by Congress for the "Watergate" crimes of conspiracy — resigned, pardoned by his successor, Vice President Gerald R. Ford. In December, with Nixon gone, the armies of the North swept across the Demilitarized Zone.

On April 28, 1975, despite fierce resistance in places by the southern army (ARVN), Saigon was completely surrounded, but with the bombardment paused to allow the remaining Americans a safe, if sorry, exit. By then, President Nguyen Van Thieu had fled the scene, later stating in our history series, "We were betrayed, stabbed, stabbed in the back." Briefly, General Duong Van "Big" Minh, who had been the third successive president I interviewed in Saigon, resumed the presidency, pleading with Washington that a negotiated settlement could still be had if the U.S. stood firm, if the Northern army faced the threat of returning B-52s.

But President Ford, in a voice of clarity so long missing, addressed the nation, saying Vietnam was "a war that has finished for America." A modest, practical man who described himself as "a Ford, not a Lincoln," he ordered a total evacuation of American military remaining in the South, and now Americans were left with the sobering, questioning sight of the last Marines in 'Nam, guardians of the U.S. Embassy, departing in helicopters taking off from the embassy roof, while desperate crowds of Vietnamese who had served the Thieu government pounded at the embassy gates, begging and bribing for a helicopter escape to the U.S. Navy ships waiting offshore.

There, the 'copter pilots watched as one by one, to make room for refugees, scores of choppers were dumped into the ocean, drowned like so many bad memories.

American historian Arthur Schlesinger would call Vietnam "the most useless, most mysterious" war. But the underlying mystery was the rigid, unchanging Washington belief in the "domino" theory, that with Sino-Soviet backing the Vietnamese "terrorists" (LBJ's description) were intent on overrunning all South-East Asia. The reality that America was intervening in a civil war, arising from the failed promises of the Geneva Accords, was essentially a taboo subject in official Washington — and for the most part in the media. Even when the Northern armies descended on Saigon, the history behind this was unknown, and un-discussed by the vast majority of the United States of America. A nation also born of nationalism, paid a heavy price for not understanding its power elsewhere.

The end came with a single symbolic tank crashing through the gates of the presidential palace, where after just three days occupancy General "Big" Minh was arrested and then, like thousands of others, sent to "re-indoctrination" camps which, however harsh, were not the predicted bloodbath. Minh was released eight years later and allowed to emigrate to France. He later moved to California, where many of the Saigon elite would settle.

The capital of the Republic of Vietnam fell after a swift offensive of just seventy-seven days, with Saigon renamed Ho Chi Minh City and the unified nation becoming the Socialist Republic of Vietnam. But though the war officially ended April 30, 1975, the Hanoi rulers postponed the victory parade to May 7 (Vietnam time), the precise date of the French defeat of May 7, 1954, at Dien Bien Phu. In so doing, the Communist victors were making clear their triumph was primarily one of Vietnamese nationalism.

This had been a very evident factor — though hard to get accepted — when I first began reporting the nature of the guerrilla nation. And Hanoi's motivating nationalism would again be dramatically evident in a new war that erupted soon after my return to Hanoi early 1979.

I had arrived on the eve of Tet, the Vietnamese lunar New Year, finding the city already packed with celebrants, everywhere calling out to each other "Chuc Mung Nam Moi" (Happy New Year). Other than all the well-wishing and the excitement of choosing traditional rice cakes and exotic flowers for loved ones and for the temple graves of ancestors, Hanoi still had the worn look of three decades of war that had only ended four years earlier. For me, the most notable change was the temporary closure of my wartime hotel, the Thong Nhat, now being totally refurbished by French financiers anticipating the tourist boom ahead. It meant I was back to the Hoa Binh, the lesser lodging where I had been unceremoniously dumped on the steps in the middle of the night after my chancy flight to Hanoi late August 1969, which now seemed centuries ago.

As a journalist, I had been privileged to report from behind the lines year after year, and now, for the first time, I was seeing Vietnam at peace — or at least a surface peace. Hanoi that Tet was a joy to see, again a city of a million inhabitants with as many more from the countryside, everywhere hugging, swaying to the beat of temple drums and what seemed the chants of a million dragon dancers.

In contrast, in this period, the U.S. and Soviet Union had been accelerating various nuclear weapons tests. Soviet and Chinese armies a million strong confronted along their national border, and just days earlier Shah Mohammad Reza Pahlavi had been driven out of Iran, soon to become an Islamic state, soon to factor in the long, futile Soviet war against the Afghan mujahideen.

In such a warring world it seemed to me then poor timing for my hoped-for television history of the entire Vietnam War, starting as World War Two ended and lasting to the recent present. Yet the concept was timely, for such a history would provide needed evidence that in our increasingly interactive world the so-called Great Powers, constantly at odds while fearing any miscalculation bringing nuclear war, were finding their many proxy wars too costly, self-defeating, and unwinnable.

But there could be no complete history of Vietnam's ten thousand days of war without full access to Hanoi's military film archives, for which I had provisional agreement subject to Politburo approval. But I would not know that decision until the three-day Tet holiday was over.

Like a good omen, Vu, my former friendly interpreter, had been assigned to me and that first day, the eve of Tet, we joined the crowds gathered around "Sword Lake" for the midnight countdown with all its prayers and promises to repent and redress all past wrongs, so that the many Gods of Tet would bestow good fortune hereafter.

One sight by the lake was astounding: couples dancing to music coming from tree-wired loudspeakers and a voice in broken English singing "Those were the days, my friend, we thought they'd never end...."

Had they ended, all those years of sacrifice? Some small part of it I had shared, and now the nostalgia of the music seized me. Alone for the three days of Tet, my mind became a spinning-top of life in and out of 'Nam, a careening of certainty and doubt.

This television history series which I called *The Ten Thousand Day War*, what were the odds of it happening? Right then, probably, ten thousand to one! Though the concept had been negotiated through my influential contact, Yasuo Yanagisawa, I had still to get Hanoi's formal approval, so I had come ten thousand miles just on chance! Would I get a curt *khong* — No. Would it matter? Yes. Without the military archives of the North there could be no complete and balanced history.

I had not only left CTV, I had consciously shed the prized role of a television news correspondent. Now, the sounds of merriment filling the city day after day merely depressed me. Had I once more been too impetuous? My seven years at CTV had been arduous but creatively rewarding. For the weekly prime-time documentary series Vice President Tom Gould had given us a free hand to choose our subjects and travels, so, on the minuscule budget of $30,000 per program — all-in right down to the paper clips — we went around the world a few times, focusing on offbeat stories usually with a moral end-sting, which viewers found enjoyable.

Financially, it was only possible by filming three or four episodes in as many countries in one swing, and then only possible because of the organizational skills of series producer Don McQueen. But the essential element was being seen on location, amid the action, and this plus conceiving, hosting, and writing twenty episodes a year, plus updating repeat-runs, took its toll.

After an exhausting four years, we suggested a Canada-focused step into the unknown: a twice-a-week live show replacing my series and that of the venerable *W5*, concentrating on hard national issues. In my role as executive producer, I thought the program appeal would be its wide-range of journalistic talent and opinion, varying from host Peter Trueman (who I "stole" from Global TV) to Barbara Amiel. I wanted to call it *The Reporters*, but CTV President Murray Chercover felt the title distracted from the news (today *Reporters* is a popular BBC series). Chercover chose the title *CTV Reports*, and in the fall of 1977 it debuted — and crashed !

The ratings sank from a million-plus for my documentary series to around 400,000 and continued down before gradually recovering, but by then after a heated exchange of insults with Chercover I had resigned (Tom Gould had left a year earlier). Yet there was really no rancour, just showbiz. In the non-subsidized world of commercial television, ratings were everything and as executive producer you delivered or died. The live tough-subject series was cancelled a few months later (though it became a guide for CBC's *The Journal*), and *W5* returned. *Maclear* did not!

But a part of me had wished for this, had perhaps brought it on, for what my sub-conscious really wanted was to produce feature-length documentaries, hopefully of lasting value, as an *independent* producer — and what better subject than the Vietnam war which had preoccupied me for so long. Now, back in Hanoi early 1979, in those lonely days of Tet listening to all the jubilation, my mental wrestling about right and wrong decisions finally quietened with the reality that there could be no room for regrets. I had staked everything on succeeding with the proposed ambitious history series.

It had to be a fully detailed history of the war presenting the views and rationale of all sides, from the return of French colonialism in 1945 to the fall of Saigon in 1975. It had to convey how swiftly the modern military machine can move and how slow and agonizing its retreat. It had to quietly document an age of great power arrogance and immorality, breeding end-less, needless war. Though the idea of undertaking a history series a mere four years after Vietnam's final offensive might have seemed somewhat early days, it was aided by the fact that there had been no extensive retrospective on the war by any of the major networks. Throughout, the viewing public had been served little more than the nightly bang-bang and the clash of pro- and anti-war factions, none of it very revealing, comforting of curing for the future.

So, Tet and torment behind me, now in the role of would-be historian, I met as pre-arranged with wartime coordinator Han Viet Tran at the Foreign Ministry. He seemed amused. "Ah, Mr. Maclear, a special welcome. Every time you come here something momentous happens. In 1969 the death of our beloved president. In 1970 the fuss over the American pris-oners. In 1972 the bombing of Hanoi. But now we're at peace. So what can possibly happen now?"

"Cambodia," I heard myself say and immediately regretted this jab. Tran was no longer smiling.

"We had no choice," he said, and I discreetly nodded.

"The Khmer Rouge were attacking our border, destroying villages, killing at random. We have film of the dead, thousands of dead. You can see for yourself in our archives."

Five weeks before, on December 25, 1978, Vietnamese infantry had invaded Cambodia, swiftly capturing Phnom Penh and driving the Khmer Rouge forces, mainly armed teenagers, to jungle hideouts bordering their ally, China. The fanatical Khmer Rouge, extreme communists led by a man-iacal parliamentarian, Pol Pot, had overthrown the government, declaring that the peasants were the new rulers. Entire urban populations had been force-marched to killing grounds where later the skulls and remains of at least a million Cambodians, upwards of a quarter of the population, were the evidence of the worst genocide since the Nazi Holocaust.

One of the victims had been a colleague and dear friend, Yoshihiko Waku, who was my cameraman during Tokyo-based years, travelling with me through most of Asia. He later joined NBC as cameraman in South Vietnam, surviving years of combat situations.

Then, on the eve of returning to his wife and two young sons in Japan, he was asked to undertake "one last" brief assignment — to Cambodia.

In May 1970, in the early phase of the Khmer Rouge uprising, Waku and NBC news Correspondent Welles Hangen drove just a few miles outside of Phnom Penh to film conditions. Taken captive, their bodies were never found.

When I last saw him, Waku-san had said to me, "Mike-san, thank you for showing me the world." I so much wish I hadn't.

Tran knew of all this, for during my December 1970 stay in Hanoi I had asked the Foreign Ministry to seek the help of Cambodia's Prince Sihanouk for information on the fate of Waku-san and others. But Sihanouk, then a prisoner in his palace, could do nothing.

Vietnam's invasion of Cambodia largely put an end to the long Khmer Rouge nightmare, but in the geopolitics of the day it was fodder for the Cold War fear that a wholly Communist Vietnam, seen as a puppet of China, would overrun the nations of South-East Asia one by one. Hanoi's action on Cambodia came at the height of the Sino-Soviet ideological split during which the United States supported China as the lesser nuclear threat.

And so with China supporting the Khmer Rouge the U.S. looked away from the Cambodian horror, while together with China condemning the Vietnam invasion.

On February 17, 1979, Tran's amused question, "What can possibly happen now?" was answered. At dawn that day, China invaded Vietnam.

At this point I had been immersed in Hanoi's military film archives for two weeks, fascinated and excited by the extremely realistic footage of all phases of the North at war since 1945. With agreement on full access to these films, and fully absorbed, I was no longer the journalist reacting to events. The old war correspondent was ready to pass on this one! But then with China's invasion came the cables. NBC and Visnews and — most important to me — CBC News wanted coverage, so on the second day of the invasion I set out for the front line of two nations who only yesterday, it seemed, had been the closest of allies.

I did not have far to go — that was the strangest part! The HQ for this new front line, Lang Son, was a mere eighty-five miles away, normally an hour's drive north of Hanoi. A sleepy provincial capital, just seven miles from the so-called "Friendship Gate" border with China, Lang Son for centuries had been the pathway for various invaders. Just getting there was a lesson in Vietnam's indifference to time; we filmed civilian refugees, whole family groups, casually heading south and platoons of infantry, some with chopsticks strapped to their loaded backsacks, slowly plodding north, as if yawning at it all.

Now, with the narrow highway jammed, the eighty-five-mile journey to Lang Son took several hours, but was perhaps the most revealing aspect of the story. At Lang Son city hall Vietnamese military PRs showed me scores of what they claimed were captured Chinese automatic rifles, though they couldn't or wouldn't provide any details on casualties. I was told that an estimated 150,000 Chinese infantry, or some fifteen divisions of the world's largest army, had spread out over several miles east to west, torching villages for what — in reference to Cambodia — Beijing called "a counterattack which the Vietnam aggressors deserve." The invaders had then halted in the hills just a mile from Lang Son city.

On a city street with a view of these hills, I reported on camera that nothing much of the nature of this war could be verified, but that the Chinese action seemed limited, mainly punitive, with neither side showing any desire to engage any further. The next day, on the very same street corner where I had stood, I was told that a Soviet news correspondent had been killed by a sniper's bullet.

But it seemed the bigger risk for me was Hanoi's reaction to my reporting. In this new war I once again used a Nihon Denpa team based in Hanoi. But cameraman Fujii had long since retired in Japan and former sound-recordist Misao Ishigaki had taken on Fujii's role, with a new soundman who played the tape of my report to the Vietnamese censor on our return to Hanoi. I was immediately summoned and rebuked for "misunderstanding" the gravity of the situation.

Then again came a rain of cables. "Maclear Hoa Binh Hotel Hanoi. Effort film hand-carried by pigeon to Bangkok. Regards Shihara (NBC Bangkok)."

"Send film to Bangkok give it to passenger — Pratt NBC Hong Kong."

"Please ignore repeat ignore earlier messages. Stop Bangkok cannot process negative stock best bet send Tokyo — regards MacDonell (Tokyo)."

"Plane late. Stuff gets out of soup to us with hour and half to bird for both CBC and NBC. If all goes well should lead both shows. MacDonell."

"Stuff was super, big raves all around. Sure you want to pull out ???????? doesn't make sense at end game. CBC and NBC willing to up ante … MacDonell."

After the trip to the front I had advised them all I could report further, if at all, only from Hanoi. There was nowhere to stay at Lang Son, no means of getting meaningful information, no means of communication from there. The better story was Hanoi's response to the war — once more, a display of ancient nationalism.

But the exchange of cables tore at me. Was I really giving up network journalism? MacDonell was right about the "end-game." To "pull out" now was most likely a life-changing decision.

Yet I hadn't returned here in the role of reporter. I was here to search Hanoi's war archives and had a deep desire to complete the search, believing it would hopefully contribute more to journalism than the nightly news reports. Foremost, I had a prior obligation to the Canadian investor group that had provided seed money for this archival undertaking, and so the "ante" was not mine to negotiate. Not least, this project might now be in danger. Hanoi had made clear to me its sensitivity about what it called the "Third Indo-China War," the first being the successful resistance to French colonial reoccupation, then the "American War," and now an invading China which might yet enlarge the danger. Certainly, priority-wise, further candid reporting from the "front" had somewhat the same risk as a sniper's bullet.

Thus far, the "Third" war hadn't escalated. There had been no use of Chinese air power or heavy artillery, and though the Chinese had an over-whelming advantage in manpower their infantry, until now, had never fought anyone. On the other hand, the Vietnamese army, perhaps the most hardened of any in the world, especially in jungle guerrilla warfare, was now largely tied up in Cambodia. So neither Vietnam nor China had any incentive to seriously engage the other, not least because Vietnam only weeks earlier had signed an "alliance" with the Soviet Union, which might conceivably get involved.

In that much, Vietnam's war of 1979 was globally of major concern. That's what had everyone on edge.

So what to do?

In particular, I welcomed the renewed relationship with CBC, whose news division was now headed by the no-nonsense, highly professional Trina McQueen, who had started as CBC's first national news woman reporter. So for a time I continued sending background reports from Hanoi.

A fascinating insight was the Hanoi street billboards which had never appeared during the "American War" but which now provided a daily summary of the face-off with China, while history-style exhibits reminded the populace that as a nation Vietnam's first war with a "rapacious" China had been in the year 111 BCE and had recurred every century or so.

The most ironic aspect was now hearing the Hanoi leadership label China in the same way the U.S. had labelled Vietnam, but with Washington now solidly on-side with Beijing. In a session with General Van Tien Dung, who had commanded the final offensive against Saigon and was now minister of defense, he referred to China's "war of expansionism" but then contemptuously dismissed it, saying "China's strength is very weak in comparison [with the war] with America" and China "will certainly meet with failure as all invaders did in the past."

Perhaps this reminder of America's recent war was not what NBC needed to hear. In one report I had said "... so much for the domino theory."

Back came a cable saying, "Would help if scripts try to stay with one idea. New York says having difficulty with wandering...."!

To my relief, China withdrew its troops on March 6 after a three-week war, for Vietnam mere seconds compared to the three decades fighting France and America. A defiant Vietnam remained in Cambodia for several more years until the forces of the apocalyptic Pol Pot had been largely decimated, though he survived in jungle border hideouts for twenty years, never brought to justice for mass genocide.

With some twenty hours of personally selected Hanoi film archives, and matching footage readily available from the American and French war archives, *Vietnam: The Ten Thousand Day War* began production late 1979 with twenty-six half-hour episodes, also versioned as thirteen one-hours, completed within one year — an astonishing achievement due to the dedication of a thirty-person team of episode producers, editors, and researchers headed by Ian McLeod as series producer and Mike Feheley as technical supervisor.

Starting production, our main concern was ensuring we had the voices of the war leaders and combatants on all sides, South and North Vietnam, France, and the United States, where we feared this entirely Canadian production might face a cold shoulder. Instead, Americans in particular, whether from high political office or of the highest military rank, as well as GI veterans of key battles, seemed anxious to unburden themselves with total candour, revealing a great many secrets and highly emotional differences on the conduct of the war.

Another main concern was that we kept to strictly non-judgmental scripting — there was to be no "enemy," just the warring sides. Unexpectedly, I wound up having to write the scripts, so always late into the night I would be choking back my personal views while Ian vetted each word for any hint of bias — by which task he ensured the objectivity of the series. The "end goal" — that future audiences could get all the facts and opinions and then make their own judgment of the war — is what still makes the series so distinct and so widely watched.

Another positive factor was that no television network had any participation whatsoever in any aspect of the series, nor would any broadcasters or distributors have any right to change the narrative. Copyright remains with the hundreds of individual Canadians who bought tax-deductible units in a public offering. Initially, PBS sought to buy U.S. rights but was declined. Instead, syndicated, it was immediately snapped up by leading regional broadcasters, almost always for prime time. In Washington, the series debuted in two-hour blocks each night for seven consecutive nights.

In Canada, CBC took the half-hour version but not all twenty-six episodes. It did not want those dealing with the French colonial era!

In France, ironically, the series was shown on a leading independent channel, and so also in the U.K. The companion book of the same title, written in 1980, was simultaneously released in the U.K, U.S., and Canada. In the U.S. the Veterans Administration acquired the series as a "therapeutic aid" for their street-front clinics, and the NEA (National Education Association), which represents all high school teachers in the U.S., chose the series as its Best Documentary for "The advancement of learning through broadcasting."

When currently Googled, "Vietnam: The Ten Thousand Day War" showed 19,100,000 "results." And yet, and yet, something was missing....

A SAM missile unit. Taken before the bombing of Hanoi in 1972.

Troops casually march, rifles and rice bowls at the ready, to the new front line with China.

In the hills near the border with China, confronting an ancient enemy.

Still searching for mines, fifty years after Dien Bien Phu.
(Photo by Michael Ellis.)

Soldiers re-enact the capture of the French HQ at Dien Bien Phu.
(Photo by Michael Ellis.)

Hanoi gets daily poster news on China's invasion.

The author at Dien Bien Phu, where the 1954 battle arena is a preserved history lesson. (Photo by Michael Ellis.)

CHAPTER FIFTEEN
Ironies

IT WOULD BE TWENTY-FOUR years before the missing piece was resolved. After the 1979 selecting of Hanoi's military archives, I did not return until 2003, with the main purpose then of filming a documentary for release on the (May 2004) fiftieth anniversary of the French defeat at Dien Bien Phu — a world-shaping event both in military and social terms, marking the collapse of colonialism in Asia, but in the Cold War era rendering new nations like bought pawns of the rival "Great Powers."

Vietnam itself was perhaps the most wounded such victim, a torn-apart country which I first visited in 1959, reporting for CBC from Saigon, and the Dien Bien Phu fiftieth anniversary coincided almost exactly with my then fifty years in Canadian television.

This would be the theme for a trilogy of feature-length documentaries for Canada's History specialty channel, looking back half a century to the makings of war in Vietnam, of apartheid in South Africa, and the rise to power of Fidel Castro in Cuba — all historic events in far different corners of the world but occurring (and filmed) at much the same time. It meant I could document a one-of-a-kind visual retrospective ranging over the lifetime of Canadian television news.

The personal recounting of this experience would be the long-felt missing part in my documentaries. I had held back my personal feelings during wartime coverage of North Vietnam, held back my personal point of view in the series *Vietnam: The Ten Thousand Day War*, but all along I felt that as the only Western network correspondent in the North several times during the war's horrific escalation, I had a need, and arguably a duty, to put on record my personal feelings. Even so, the reality of such filming was possible only because of the unhesitating support of History channel head of factual programming John Gill and his successor Cindy Witten, herself an ex-CBC journalist, who patiently nursed and helped guide the project.

This time I had come to Vietnam with a globally experienced Canadian crew, cameraman Mike Ellis and sound technician John Martin, and the result would be the stunning photography and effects in the film *Vietnam: Ghosts of War*. But arriving in Hanoi after a gap of twenty-four years I had to first adjust to the new Vietnam of the twenty-first century, the great majority of its population born since the war, a nation that had "moved on," its Hollywood-minded youth only faintly interested in the long, controversial war of attrition that had so totally divided the world generations before.

Returning to Hanoi was a joyous-sad experience, a city quite new to me of grand hotels and international boutiques, but sadly my Vietnamese contacts from the wartime years had all gone, their whereabouts or fate unknown to my young new "minders." How I missed the sensitive, inquisitive Vu! Tran, having risen high in the Foreign Ministry, had long since retired, but where no one seemed to know. The ministry's priorities had changed, still cooperative but somewhat indifferent, its assistance ruled by the dollars it could extract, which, as in the new China, was the main preoccupation of Vietnam's modern communism. An exception was VTV, its staff mostly as young as Vietnam television, all of them I met familiar with *The Ten Thousand Day War*, which they had in their archives, though how acquired I did not ask. I would also find the companion book on display in stores, the pirated English version aimed at tourists but with a pirated Chinese translation familiar to any interested Vietnamese. But then American outlets — Amazon, YouTube, and various Google offerings — had long since been either showing or selling pirated versions. Vietnam was merely joining a digital world in which copy replaced copyright!

For me, with so many ingrained memories of wartime Hanoi, the newly risen city was at first sight surreal. The once calm streets full of silently gliding bikes were now a ceaseless roar of Honda-hogs, the cyclists once so gracious now all masked against pollution and looking like the end of days; my old hotel Thong Nhat now the French-renovated

Metropole with a lobby gourmet store of fine delicacies and wines which for me simply couldn't match the nightly stale chicken and obligatory Tiger beer of a reporter's past.

I wanted to revisit the POW camp where I had filmed on Christmas Day 1970, long before my young minder was born.

"Ah," he said, "Hanoi Hilton," and he took me to the Hoa Lo in downtown Hanoi, now a tourist attraction where one pays to enter prison! When I told him this wasn't the camp I filmed he insisted there was only ever one POW camp. "Hanoi Hilton," he repeated. He was clearly offended. Did I, a foreigner, know better than him, a native of Hanoi? Finally, after describing in detail the layout and distinctive willow pond at the camp I'd filmed he recognized it as the current Ministry of Information film editing facility (mostly young editors working in the one-time "cells" where the iron bars on the windows still remained). And when walking away from the Hoa Lo my minder found no irony in turning the street corner and seeing there a real, newly opened Hanoi Hilton.

More pleasing were the sights outside of Hanoi, especially along Highway 1, which in the bomb-cratered year 1969 had taken me weeks to traverse in an unforgettable jolting jeep, but which now in a brand new Land Rover was a smooth half a day's ride. The one time B-52 devastation now seemed impossible to believe — but for the record of our films at that time! Everywhere, new towns lined the highway with no architectural resemblance to those of yesteryear, mostly looking like heaps of brick piled at all angles and devoid of charm, but still home sweet home in a free land. Some discoveries were unexpected — the daily lines a thousand strong of families filing into the mausoleum of Ho Chi Minh, three decades after his death; Hanoi's numerous specialty universities, one teaching nine languages; and the tourism.

A surprise was the high proportion of American tourists, since successive U.S. administrations and big business had been so slow to either aid or trade with the new modern-minded Vietnam, already a member of the World Trade Organization and with a population exceeding 91,000,000, almost double that of the two partitioned Vietnams. Surprisingly, I saw American tourists among the long queue of mourners at the Ho Chi Minh mausoleum, others at the city's war museum, for the most part GI veterans here with their now-adult sons and daughters en route to the notorious battle grounds in the South such as Khe Sanh, a remote high-plateau fire-base near the partition line where the early 1968 siege of five thousand U.S. Marines modelled that of the trapped French force at Dien Bien Phu fourteen years before, in each case a major factor in turning the public against the war.

It would be a much better history lesson if the returning GIs went first to Dien Bien Phu! From Hanoi's sparkling new self-built Noi Bai airport, it is just an hour's flight on Air Vietnam or Tiger Airways to the battleground that would herald the end of foreign military dominance in Asia. How that came about in 1954 and the repetition of self-defeating Great Power arrogance which remains constant would be the theme of a documentary intended as an outspoken sequel to *Vietnam: The Ten Thousand Day War*.

Imagine a time when there was just one American soldier in Vietnam! At that time, in the last days of World War Two, Major Archimedes Patti, an intelligence officer with the OSS (forerunner of the CIA) had been on a covert mission. He had been sent to contact Viet Minh rebels who, having all along resisted French colonialism, were now grouping in the northern mountainous forests in the region of Dien Bien Phu, awaiting the defeat of the Japanese occupation.

Patti's mission was to enlist Viet Minh assistance in rescuing any American pilots shot down along the Vietnam-China border. It was there that he sought out a mystical figure who had many aliases but was known to his followers as "The General," an old man with a goatee, khaki shorts held up by string, and worn-out sandals. Ho Chi Minh's "perfect" English surprised Patti. The two men also, despite their age difference, shared the bond of a hard-fought life. Like Ho, Patti, a New Yorker born to poor Italian immigrants, was a fierce patriot, having performed covert missions in North Africa and in Sicily and Salerno, and having been with the invading forces preparing to liberate all of his native land when he was told of his new assignment in Asia.

While knowing that Ho was a communist, Patti supported the views of President Franklin D. Roosevelt that the colonial powers driven from Asia should not be allowed to return. So there was an instant trust between the major and the "General." Interviewed for *The Ten Thousand Day War*, Patti remembered that he first met Ho "on the last day of April, 1945," and it was on that same day thirty years later that the last American soldiers would leave Vietnam. Between those dates, some six million GIs would see war service in Vietnam. Some 58,000 of them would die there, as well as two million Vietnamese.

The first American soldier in Vietnam might have prevented the tragedy of those ten thousand days — had he been heeded!

Patti would be the earliest U.S. intelligence officer knowledgeable about Ho Chi Minh's background, and he referred to Ho as being "no die-hard communist."

When they met, Ho had only recently returned to Vietnam, having left his country forty years before, after reasoning that colonialism could only be defeated by opposition within the democracies. At age twenty-one, he set out as a galley hand on a French merchant ship bound for London, there finding work as an assistant chef at the Carlton Hotel while founding an anti-colonial group called the Overseas Workers Association. Briefly, travelling as a deck hand, he spent a winter in New York, shovelling snow for a meagre living in Harlem, then in 1919 after the end of World War One he moved to France, seeking to influence Indo-China's colonial master. Using the name Nguyen Ai Quoc (Nguyen the Patriot) he became editor of a newspaper for exiles, *La Paria* — The Outcast. While working as a laundry washer, and already fluent in French, he co-founded the French Communist Party.

In 1922, Ho travelled to Moscow as a delegate of the Communist International then stayed for two years studying Marxist doctrine, earning him a position as aide to the Soviet consulate in Canton (Guangzhou), China. For the next twenty years, using various alliances, Ho travelled through South-East Asia recruiting Vietnamese exiles such as history teacher Vo Nguyen Giap and mandarin intellectual Pham Van Dong. In early 1945 they and others regrouped in southern China, but then Ho was quickly imprisoned by Chiang Kai shek's Kuomintang party at the time of bitter, prolonged civil war with Mao Zhedong's communist forces.

Ironically, the U.S., which then had an "observer mission" in China assessing both sides of the civil war, insisted on Ho's release, seeing him as a more reliable adviser than the French on the future of Indo-China. And with Ho's release the fledgling "League for the Independence of Vietnam" — popularly known as the Viet Minh — relocated in the far northern jungles of Vietnam, where OSS Major Patti was assigned to seek out their support.

Ho readily agreed to assist the U.S., saying he hoped for "America's future recognition." Ho confided his fear that the quisling French-backed emperor Bao Dai, kept in power first by Vichy France and then by the occupying Japanese, would be the rationale for France to re-occupy rubber-rich Vietnam after the defeat of Japan.

Even after the collapse of Nazi Germany, with the Pacific war still undetermined, Roosevelt was leaning toward the idea of a new United Nations acting as trustee of former Asian colonies, pending the time and means of their independence.

But President Roosevelt died on April 12, 1945, just days before Major Patti arrived in Vietnam, and with Roosevelt's passing and U.S. concern about Soviet seizure of eastern Europe, the demands of the colonial powers prevailed. Following the unconditional surrender of imperial Japan, it meant the swift return of colonial armies to Indo-China, Indonesia, Burma, and India.

In the brief interim, Patti was with Ho as the rag-tag Viet Minh briefly occupied the capital, Hanoi, where Ho publicly announced a Declaration of Independence, its preamble (aided by Patti) word for word that of the United States. As Patti told it, "The crowd was fantastic. Ho was very anxious for America's recognition, saying again and again, 'We want nothing else, just moral support.'"

For a time, he got it. Patti was instructed to help train Viet Minh units in the use of modern arms. But in that fall of 1945 French troops, which had first seized Vietnam in 1858, later annexing Laos and Cambodia, returned in force with no protest from the administration of President Harry Truman. The Viet Minh were forced to retreat to hill forests beyond Dien Bien Phu while gradually organizing guerrilla warfare against French-held urban areas.

In a complete reversal of Roosevelt's ideas, the U.S. then began increasingly financing the French army of occupation. Even so, the Viet Minh guerrilla tactics wore down not only the French army but also the French public. After nine years culminating at the battle of Dien Bien Phu, France completely withdrew from Vietnam.

After the same number of combat years, exhausted by the same guerrilla tactics, the U.S. in turn withdrew from Vietnam.

The main historical evidence — and lessons — of those wars is the battleground of Dien Bien Phu, where fifty years later we filmed *Vietnam:*

Ghosts of War. I had been to this remote northwest corner of Vietnam once before, during my first 1969 filming in North Vietnam. What started out as a day trip lasted three days because of the area's notorious sudden fog, a big factor in the French defeat. On that visit, staying at a guest lodge on a hilltop called Eliane, one of ring of firebases the French had named after their ladies back home, I could view the entire historic battlefield. For days during the recurring fogs I sat on the guest house terrace, Tiger beer in hand, trying to imagine that on this very hill several hundred French and Vietnamese had fought so valiantly, hand-to-hand like ancient gladiators accepting death in the name of national honour. It occurred to me then that Dien Bien Phu could be a telling documentary on lessons unlearned. In a last desperate tactic after nine years of uncontainable guerrilla warfare, the French had gambled on luring the Viet Minh into open battle, as the American military later hoped to do.

The French high command in Hanoi selected the valley of Dien Bien Phu ("Arena of the Gods"), with its sole northern road link to Laos, as a supply route the Viet Minh in the surrounding hills had to defend at all costs. The danger for the French was that Dien Bien Phu, though just 170 miles from Hanoi, was accessible only by air. They would need to swiftly occupy the valley and then build a runway and army barracks. In Hanoi, twelve thousand paratroopers and technical personnel — the cream of the French army in Vietnam — were readied, to be dispatched in stages. On November 30, 1953, three hundred men of the First Colonial Paratroop Battalion boarded an American C-47 waiting for the "Go" signal from a scout plane ensuring that the valley, as usual, was unoccupied and safe.

But the fog was heavy that day. For two hours the scout plane patrolled the area and was about to turn back when the fog suddenly lifted and the "Go" signal, "Texas," a bow to U.S. military support, was sent.

The French high command had decided that the seizing of Dien Bien Phu, which in 1887 had been the last and most testing part of Vietnam to be subjugated, was to be a now-or-never venture. If the air drop didn't succeed at once the Viet Minh would certainly be waiting in ambush for any second attempt.

For the paratroopers, the valley with its narrow six-mile trail leading to Laos looked like the handle of a giant frying pan — and into it they jumped!

Now, back in Dien Bien Phu for a documentary on the fiftieth anniversary of the French surrender, the remoteness of the place had its own magic — and frustrations. It was still only reachable from Hanoi by air, except for hiking village to village through Vietnam's far northwest. So we had flown in to the very same airstrip where West fought East — and lost.

The physical reminders of the battle were immediately gripping, though the living conditions at the small nearby town would be a day-by-day depression. Our three-man film crew had been the only foreigners on the crowded flight, full of local tradesmen who were evidently regular visitors to Hanoi seeking something edible! At the one recommended hotel the meals were a necessity like the toilet, but not to be discussed. On arrival, the first sight was that of a long suffering cockerel, its legs bolted to the cement entry, its howl an unnerving 4 a.m. awakening each day with the first rays of the sun.

But, film-perfect, the valley battlefield had been preserved like an apt open-air theatre of war. Shell-pocked tanks and twisted cannon still lined the runway where we'd landed, sappers still swept the fields for landmines, the French battle HQ with its underground quarters and corrugated roof was exactly as when abandoned half a century before, the miles of deep World War One-style trenches the Viet Minh had dug for the final offensive had survived the decades — an appealing sight for historians and mosquitos — but on the seven hilltop firebases, with their ill-fitting feminine names, elephant grass now disguised the horror where thousands died.

For the filming, we had brought three Vietnamese generals with us, all veterans of Dien Bien Phu. Needing high-angle shots of the battleground, we decided to climb firebase "Beatrice," where the bloodiest of the bayonet fighting had occurred, now totally covered by elephant grass taller than any man.

Our generals, well into their eighties, shinnied effortless to the top. Led by our young minder, cameraman Mike Ellis and soundman John Martin unhesitatingly followed. At seventy-five, with a damaged hip, I had to mount Beatrice or go home! Grasping at the thick grass roots, it took a good twenty minutes to haul myself to the top, there to be greeted by sardonic clapping.

From the-top of Beatrice, the generals could point out for us the distant heights where we'd film General Vo Nguyen Giap's jungle head-quarters, while explaining the Viet Minh strategy for victory. Largely invisible despite constant aerial surveillance, the Viet Minh could watch every move the French made, seeing the build-up of troops and arms and realizing that to engage the French would be suicidal. Though far superior in manpower, the scattered Viet Minh forces were woe-fully inferior in firepower. Like the French, the priority for Giap was the coming Geneva meeting of the Great Powers scheduled for May 8, 1954, specifically to resolve the issue, or conduct, of colonialism in Indo-China. As the French commander in Hanoi, General Henri Navarre, described it to us, "The Viet Minh understood that if the French could be seriously defeated at Dien Bien Phu this would allow them, polit-ically, to win the war. So they decided to take all the risks."

In fact, with the agreement of Ho Chi Minh, Giap had decided there should be no gamble. The defeat of the French had to be total or the Viet Minh could never hope to drive out the colonialists. In early 1954, with five months remaining until Geneva, Giap decided on a series of skir-mishes, nothing too serious but enough to keep the French convinced that these were the probes for the big face-to-face engagement they wanted. As he would do in the subsequent "American war," Giap drafted all available civilians, mostly women and youths, to assist his troops in forging a jungle supply route stretching 450 kilometres from the border with China. In what would be a blueprint for the future war with America, this all-people guerrilla force physically dug rough roads and mountain trails, camouflaged for the Molotov trucks and the thousands of *xe tho* pack-bikes bringing supplies and weapons to the waiting Viet Minh at Dien Bien Phu.

According to the generals we had brought there, over the last steep fifty kilometres everything had to be hand-hauled up the mountains, and this included what the French commanders had thought impossible: so-called "steel elephants" or 105mm cannon, the equal or better of the French artillery.

One of our veteran generals, who had been in charge of conscript morale, demonstrated through hand movements how teams of youths, yoked with ropes to the big guns, had dragged them inch by inch, a few herculean yards each day, to the camouflaged forest caves overlooking the valley of Dien Bien Phu.

Placed on wood-based rollers, easily moved in or out of the caves, the lethal guns were invisible to the French force far below. Giap now had two hundred of the 105mm guns and some eight hundred lighter recoilless cannon, according to our veteran guides. Two very different types of warfare were about to be tested at Dien Bien Phu: conventional vs. guerrilla war *on guerrilla territory*, as would be the case in the "American War" to follow and again currently in Afghanistan.

At dusk, March 12, 1954, Giap's heavy guns all at once fired on the unsuspecting colonial army, with the vital airstrip destroyed in the first moments. Against a blinding sun the French could not locate Giap's guns even when they were firing. The barrage lasted until sunset, for the French an eternity during which the senior artillery officer committed suicide with a hand grenade.

Simultaneously, Viet Minh infantry stormed the supposedly protective firebases, the fighting so fierce that reportedly in the first hours five hundred French and as many or more Viet Minh troops died on Beatrice alone.

The battle of Dien Bien Phu would rage on for fifty-five days until it became hand-to-hand trench warfare on a scale unequalled since World War One. The French surrender on May 7, 1954, came just one day before the U.S., USSR, Great Britain, and France met at Geneva, but essentially the battle was lost that first day nearing the Ides of March, after nine years of guerrilla war. It would be a March day in 1965 when the first U.S. combat troops went ashore at China Beach, Da Nang, and nine years later, February 1973, when U.S. forces left Vietnam, officially reunited on May 7, 1975.

The test of both wars — that of France and America — was that of a different generation of Viet Minh overcoming its adversary by infiltrating superior manpower, using the same jungle-trail means learned at Dien Bien Phu.

So for their part, what had the Great Powers learned?

The French, with the loss of three thousand men and as many more permanently disabled, and with all those that could walk force-marched to prison camps five hundred miles away (an ordeal that only one in two of them would survive) abandoned Indo-China and to their great credit supported the May 8, 1954 Geneva Accords partitioning Vietnam but providing for national elections within two years.

Only one country abstained: the United States, which, having chosen as the new ruler of the South a long-time absentee, Ngo Dinh Diem, a Catholic in a country ninety-five percent Buddhist, found itself taking sides in a civil war which increasingly became a proxy war with the early Sino-Soviet alliance.

"Why Vietnam?" would become the unanswered mystery that divided a nation and tarnished the legacies of four successive presidents: Dwight Eisenhower, John Kennedy, Lyndon Johnson, and Richard Nixon.

Why Vietnam? Because despite Kennedy's borrowed words that America had nothing to fear but fear itself, all those presidents found fear politically convenient, lending them the profile of strong men saving America from perceived danger, unreal in the case of Vietnam's civil war, arising from betrayal of the Geneva Accords.

The great mystery of the Vietnam War is how the United States, with the benefit of what France had experienced, would engage in a war in which it knew almost nothing of the supposed enemy. Simply put, perceptions — not reality — guided each president.

Eisenhower, the loveable Ike who helped liberate Europe from fascism, would finance 80 percent of the nine-year doomed French colonial war on the perception the U.S. was helping contain expansionist communism.

Kennedy, who so accurately analyzed the nature of people's war, nevertheless committed the first American military advisers, which would lead to nine years of U.S. combat — and further defeat.

Johnson, as a rationale for American combat, would deceive the Congress he previously led and would deny the American public any knowledge of the extent and nature of the undeclared war with the North.

Nixon, elected on a vow of peace, instead enlarged the war — and civilian tragedy — by secretly invading Cambodia, paving the way for the Khmer Rouge. In turn, in self-wasting wars, the U.S. would invade Iraq on the perception it had weapons of mass destruction, and then Afghanistan on the perception it was the root of terrorism — wars that would both end indecisively, though at a crippling cost for the American people.

In the case of Vietnam, time would prove there had been no justification, the early personal conclusion I now sought to document in

Vietnam: Ghosts of War. In *Vietnam: The Ten Thousand Day War*, the objective was to present all points of view on the war, to be a future reference of the mindset of the political leaders, military chiefs, and combatants. But almost a quarter of a century after that series, with the interval one of so much war and fear, it felt right to be back at Dien Bien Phu, where the cycle of questionable great power wars began. *Ghosts of War* would be a journalist's eyewitness conclusion that had no part in the history series.

However important, by its very format that series was inconclusive, mainly revealing how little was learned. At Dien Bien Phu, one of our veteran generals bluntly said on camera "America never understood Vietnamese nationalism — that was America's biggest mistake." Then General Giap himself telling us, quoting Ho Chi Minh after the victory at Dien Bien Phu, "Now we have America to face." So many voices seemed to echo through the valley of Dien Bien Phu as we filmed: U.S. field commander General William Westmoreland unwittingly revealing the total misunderstanding of guerrilla war, saying, "Throughout the war we never lost a battle"; South Vietnam's General Nguyen Van Thieu saying over and over, "We didn't lose — we were betrayed," but his vice president Nguyen Cao Ky saying, "America's fault was in doing too much for us." There was America's most senior general, Maxwell Davenport Taylor, unequivocally regretting the Vietnam War. "We didn't know our ally. Secondly, we knew even less about the enemy. And last, most inexcusable of our mistakes, was not knowing our own people."

At the same time, foreseeing a very different future, there was Secretary of State Dean Rusk saying "The leadership of some future war will have to consider whether maximum force be used at the very beginning; put in a stack of blue chips."

Yet the unlearned lesson was that superior firepower did not prevail in Vietnam, nor in the wars to follow, so seemingly in future there was no quick solution unless the blue chips were to be nuclear.

Vietnam: Ghosts of War is a film about the power of militant nationalism, which, however disturbing, has to be accommodated, not eliminated. A united Vietnam, which had been possible without thirty years of war, was ultimately to prove no threat to anyone — a respected, somewhat inward-looking nation, albeit communist.

When the film had its theatrical debut at the world renowned Hot Docs festival, after viewing it the then-head of the National Film Board asked me which was the most important documentary — *Ghosts* or *The Ten Thousand Day War*.

"Oh, the latter," I somewhat automatically responded.

"I'm not so sure," he said.

CHAPTER SIXTEEN
The Unimaginable

IN APRIL 2010, AS part of the ceremonies marking the thirty-fifth anniversary of Vietnam's reunification, the state network VTV (Vietnam Television) made a request I could never have imagined. It wanted to broadcast, unchanged on its documentary channel, the entire thirteen hours of *Vietnam: The Ten Thousand Day War*, and asked if I would come to Hanoi to introduce the series.

My first inclination at age eighty was to plead a horror of flying (true), a loss of words (increasingly true), and a loathing of mass transit motorbikes (absolutely true). But I agreed conditionally on the principle that I paid my own costs, and with a request of my own — that VTV arrange interviews with the key generals for a potential film history of the war on the Ho Chi Minh Trail, still a little known but decisive factor in Vietnam's guerrilla war with America.

VTV agreed and when meeting in Hanoi further agreed to a co-production role, providing non-editorial assistance such as transportation, guides, interpreters, secondary camera crew, and clearance of still-unreleased military footage of the longest, strangest, and most successful guerrilla war in modern times. The idea for a feature-length history of the Trail had been on my mind for some time, though I couldn't really imagine it happening. Now VTV's signed participation made the logistics far less formidable. I felt confident of finding Canadian and U.S. broadcaster funding, and of returning soon with a film crew! At this point, my extended Vietnam visits, both South and North, covered more than fifty years. Just one more time, I told myself!

Adding to the appeal and importance of the project, interviews with the two most experienced military commanders on the Trail vividly brought to life its unique decade-long warfare, fought under unimaginable conditions. With overall commander General Dong Si Nguyen I first had to test how forthcoming and candid he would be, so I started with what was perhaps — for the history books — the key question: How many troops went down the Trail? Two million, he replied — an astonishing number far beyond U.S. intelligence estimates. All these years later, General Nguyen could afford at times to sound cavalier. "The more they hit us with B-52s the more troops we sent in!

"Our people have had the tradition, through many generations, that we never surrender to anybody, any bigger nation." It meant from the start "preparing for a long-term war" and with Vietnam partitioned and with the tactics of Dien Bien Phu as the model, the North knowingly set out to create what it officially called "the Truong Son strategic supply route," but which the U.S. military labelled "The Ho Chi Minh Trail."

"We defied the Americans. I'm not trying to exaggerate here. We defied them because they invaded Vietnam and that made our sacrifice justifiable." How great was the sacrifice, especially during the Trail's formative years? "In the early years, from the year 1959 to 1962, supplies to the South were carried on foot, using labour forces. But the supply task was extremely difficult due to air attacks and jungle weather, and we suffered large casualties in those years."

Late in 1963, with the military slaying of Saigon's President Diem followed by the assassination of President John F. Kennedy, the North, fearing an enlarged war, decided to "escalate" on its terms, sending regular troops down the Trail, some by truck, but these were "very few and we met with so many obstacles. There were days, even weeks when we got stuck in some place, not able to move at all. There were days we lost hundreds of our soldiers.

"In the early years that our troops moved into the South, we walked! Walking and carrying forty kilograms for each person, plus rifles. They had to climb very high mountains, even where there were no footpaths, climbing the cliffs. But the soldiers had been well trained before going South, and we had prepared medicines for our soldiers. For all situations. Got a snake bite? Mosquitoes? There's medicine for it right away.

Terrestrial leeches? There's special soap to deal with it. But the greatest hardship of all in those early days was walking while having to carry so much heavy stuff, and in the first four years, getting North to South took the soldiers many months. Later it took only seven days. That's what defeated America!"

His personal challenge? "The thing which always held tight on my mind, day and night, was how to meet the demands for all the seven battlefields in seven directions [of the Trail], including Vietnam, Laos, and Kampuchea [Cambodia]." This was the first revelation of the number of regional speciality armies on the Trail.

Today, General Nguyen is in overall command of a great commemorative highway stretching along the western slopes of the Ho Chi Minh Trail, North to South for six hundred kilometres. Entirely Vietnamese-built, it should be ready by the spring 2015 fiftieth anniversary of the war's end. As the general put it, "We had to continue with what we inherited from history." The official purpose is to protect the topography of the Truong Son range and create a new unified economic region linking railroads, hydro, factories, and farmland to serve the whole country.

But this new Trail, with so much bitter history and contrasting botanical beauty, is also likely to become one of the world's great tourist attractions, with battle landmarks all along its route. Jokingly, I asked the general, "Will there be motels, restaurants, McDonalds, Burger Kings?" and he said "We wish for all of those. This road will welcome everybody, any business. We wish for friendship."

Back at the hotel, I felt even more certain that a feature-length documentary on the history of the Trail would be a war story unlike any other. For seldom, if ever in our times, had a war ended with so little rancour and such fast recovery — at least for Vietnam. I began carefully organizing my notes, including the interview with Transport Division Commander on the Trail, Colonel Pham Huu Dai, who would reveal what has been arguably the best kept secret of the Vietnam War — until now!

I had asked him "Were you ever in doubt?" and then he told of a time unimaginable, when the North feared "all seemed lost."

For ten years as commander of the vital truck divisions supplying the troops infiltrating south, he had lived on the Ho Chi Minh Trail, every day enduring the heaviest air bombardment in the history of warfare. For a thousand aerial miles, all through the sixties, the sky above, he recalls, was "layered with death," with U.S. airpower typically stacked at different tactical heights, first the A-26 and T-28 propeller spotter craft, then A-7 and A-54 reconnaissance jets, then F-4, F-100, and F-105 Phantom jet fighters, then KC-135 refuelling tankers and EC-130 operations command aircraft, then B-52 "Fortress" bombers and perhaps SR-71 "Blackbird" stealth reconnaissance. Only the natural camouflage of the mountainous jungle, increasingly defoliated, protected the trucks and troops on the Trail.

Then, in early 1971, ironically at the height of U.S. troop withdrawal from the South, a single aircraft assigned over the Trail threatened its defenders as never before, the colonel told me. Whereas previously, in his words, it took " squadrons" of fighter-bombers using "tons of bombs" to track and attack a truck convoy, the low-flying AC-130, equipped with thermo-imaging, could lock onto its prey, circle a convoy, and mortally shell the trucks one by one.

In his living room the colonel suddenly stood, thrusting out his arms, fists clenched like so many sidewinders, his voice imitating the sound of fire from the AC-130: "Tak-ang, Tak-ang," echoing through the forest "like some furious monster."

Swiftly, the extent of losses became greater than "we could make up in time." As he described it, it was "a time of utter confusion," the truck run to the South now suicidal.

At an emergency meeting of divisional chiefs, overall commander General Dong Sy Nguyen told them that in continuing to take chances they were "doomed to failure." He decided on a total halt to all infiltration until new, massively camouflaged routes could be mapped and completed.

As Colonel Dai related to me, half a million troops were assigned to a "herculean task" approached as "a matter of life or death" for the North. It meant digging up tens of thousands of jungle trees from impassable regions, then transplanting them in wall-to-wall form on both sides of new truck routes with dense cover-all roofing. And it meant a reversal of past tactics, a switch to daytime runs so as to have some light for the drivers, but "within one month" the amazing task was finished and the new runs "succeeded."

I asked what the North considered the most decisive battle of the war in the South and without any hesitation he said "Khe Sanh."

This was the siege of a 1477-foot hilltop firebase, with a plateau large enough to have an airstrip, in the far northeast below the demilitarized zone and bordering on the Trail. Here in early 1967 U.S. Marines had seized the one-time French fortification as a base for forward patrols to monitor "NV" infiltration and for deterrent commando raids.

Like Dien Bien Phu, to which Khe Sanh at first seemed similar, nothing much happened for several months and the Marine force was expanded to 5,600 men. Then on January 1968, in the dense forests where reconnaissance planes could see very little, acoustic sensors began to detect heavy troop movement, soon identified as two elite divisions, one — the 304th — the same division that had led the first assault on the French firebases at Dien Bien Phu. Now as then, some twenty thousand North Vietnamese troops with heavy cannon had the marines outnumbered and outgunned. At dawn on January 21, long-range artillery struck the firebase with deadly accuracy, crippling the airstrip and killing fifteen Marines in the first salvo.

But tactically Khe Sanh was no Dien Bien Phu. The U.S. had total air power and from the start the adjacent forest became a napalm inferno, code-named Operation Niagara to convey the ceaseless rain of bombs. Even so, undetected deep in the forest, the artillery fire continued unabated, with the Marines dependent on supplies parachuted in and with the wounded having no airlift out. But even with so many Marines trapped, the U.S. decided it must hold Khe Sanh or risk a humiliating setback, so the siege would rage on for seventy-seven days until, just as suddenly as it began, the NV seemed to melt away. Day after day, the fate of Khe Sanh dominated the news, and for an alarmed American public anything worse in Vietnam was unimaginable.

As Colonel Dai explained it, the North judged success in the South by "gateways" and Khe Sanh was "the number one Gateway" because it enabled the "Tet Offensive." At around 2 a.m. on January 31, 1968, the start of the Vietnamese Lunar New Year — The Year of the Monkey — with the diversion of Khe Sanh still raging, a largely Viet Cong force disguised as vendors and soldiers on leave simultaneously stormed a hundred provincial capitals and towns, in Saigon taking the fight to the very compound of the United States embassy. The Tet Offensive itself was brief and suicidal for most of the attackers, but its brazenness and total surprise rocked the U.S. administration and the American public to the extent that President Johnson that year decided he would not seek re-election.

The new Ho Chi Minh highway is to curl close to Khe Sanh, which in terms of a nation's demoralization was indeed another Dien Bien Phu.

Leaving the colonel, I had fought my way through the Hanoi streets of today, facing the threatening legions of Hondas and Yamahas and Kawasakis and Suzukis, for me their roar more startling than any mere "Tak-ang, Tak-ang"!

Yet of all the memories of 'Nam perhaps the strangest was on this last 2010 visit to Hanoi, back at the hotel just in time to turn on VTV's documentary channel and see an episode ("Westy's War") from *Vietnam: The Ten Thousand Day War*. I watched the once-unimaginable, awed by the fact the Vietnamese state network was showing a foreign-produced history of the entire thirty-year war, but stunned even more by the sight of U.S. field commander General William Westmoreland, in a deadpan tone, reciting Kipling:

> *The end of the fight is a tombstone white,*
> *With the name of the late deceased.*
> *And the epitaph drear, a fool lies here,*
> *Who tried to hustle the East.*

The author with General Dong Si Nguyen, overall commander of the Trail.

The author with Colonel Dai, commander of the supply trucks infiltrating south.

Hauling a network of pipes down the Trail — a major key to victory.

Northern troops infiltrate the southern delta.

The beginning of the end: storming the demilitarized zone.

NV troops guard palace grounds after Saigon's surrender.

North Vietnamese navigate a river to infiltrate south, circa 1964–65.

Epilogue

THOUGH THE CAST OF those early days at the "Network" remain vivid in my mind, for the most part I have had no communication with them in the decades since. Of Management in the sixties and early seventies, it can be said that they kept their heads in the sand! External factors, not self-reform, very gradually forced radical change and in my judgment it would be the late seventies before CBC warranted national trust with a succession of remarkable heads of TV programming, notably Peter Herrndorf, Trina McQueen, Ivan Fecan who, however, all chose to eventually leave. Today CBC's creative talent — especially in News — is, or should be, the subject of national pride.

Some of the old management, once freed of their clan, I would hear from. TV Foreign news manager Ron Robbins retired to become dean of a prairie university, where years later he kindly offered me a chair in journalism; Peter Trueman moved to Global TV as news anchor and later hosted the short lived *CTV Reports*, which became my last venture as a network staffer; Don MacDonald, some five years after I left CBC, in a lengthy public mea culpa stated his regrets and said what happened was CBC's loss.

Knowlton Nash, who first made his mark at CBC reporting from Washington to *Newsmagazine*, eventually side-stepped senior management, becoming anchor of the nightly newscast *The National*, though the credit for that title is due to correspondent William "Bill" Cunningham.

For many years Knowlton and I maintained a strained friendship. I would meet with him and his wife Lorraine Thomson, herself a media personality, at their home for New Year's brunch. We never once discussed what had happened or what might have been.

As for John Kerr, having so suddenly taken over the management of TV news, he just as suddenly seemed to fade from view.

Knowlton's dream project, *Weekend*, the Saturday and Sunday combo news and current Affairs program I had abandoned, came to an early end, the Saturday edition lasting one year, the Sunday edition just two. But it had one notable success: the "girl" reporter it sought proved to be its outstanding talent — Catherine Margaret (Trina) Janitch, who married TV producer Don McQueen, would help usher in a new era of progressive management, first heading TV news, then becoming head of all factual programming. She had that rare talent of spotting and promoting other talent such as Brian Stewart and Peter Mansbridge, and as chief correspondent and host of *The National* Mansbridge in turn has helped forge an exceptional news team (nightly challenged by CTV's populist chief anchor Lisa Laflamme), with Mark Starowicz the equivalent heading CBC non-News documentaries. Trina, after leaving CBC to head CTV and then launching highly successful specialty channel Discovery Canada would discover not least a wealth of independent journalists and producers. Overall, it was the later management at CBC which demonstrated how hapless the earlier management had been.

Newsmagazine live, the first news background program which Morley Safer and I shaped, would quickly become the test ground for bright new producers, correspondents and hosts, notably Tom Gould, William Cunningham, Don Cameron, Craig Oliver, Joan Donaldson, Peter Kent, Henry Champ, and Lloyd Robertson, all of whom except Bill would eventually take that walk up Toronto's Jarvis Street to the no-nonsense environment of CTV. *Newsmagazine* would endure almost thirty years until replaced by *The Journal*, then by *the fifth estate*.

Of that early talent, the CBC's mostly senseless loss was that of Morley Safer. When *Newsmagazine* had to choose a new host, Morley — then in charge — insisted that it be a journalist, while management insisted on a staff announcer. Morley tendered his resignation and CBC casually let go the best overall news talent it ever had, then typically years later had second thoughts and re-hired Morley as London correspondent, only to lose him to CBS, where he became a star of *60 Minutes*.

Of my colleagues in Vietnam, cameraman Ryoko Fujii survived — and filmed — the 1972 bombing of Hanoi, then retired somewhere on the

Tokaido route between Tokyo and Kyoto, fittingly the realm of the Samurai warriors. Soundman Misao Ishigaki became head of Nihon Denpa News, whose founder Yasuo Yanagisawa remained a dear apolitical friend until his death at ninety-one.

As for me, looking back on the early years at CBC, I feel privileged to have had some part in its journalistic evolution, and also with that of CTV — in total, twenty-five years with the two networks — but just as privileged to have had a role in the blossoming of independent documentary productions for the past thirty-five years. So much of the very best Canadian film and journalistic talent would be found, and should be found outside the networks, and I was fortunate to work with the best of these.

Of course, in one's mind the golden years are always those of years past, and in the fast, shifting world of television programming to remain mentally in the past, or even to be perforce absent from the present for some years, is to find yourself suddenly out of touch. Perhaps mercifully! That last documentary I had been so confident about, a first television history of the Ho Chi Minh Trail, never came about.

Despite my contacts and past productions, the various history channels weren't doing history anymore — at least as I knew it. Perhaps if I had animated the troops going down the Trail and piled on the sound-tracks along with the bombs, if I had adapted to the style of *Tank Wars* or borrowed from *Storage Wars* or *Pawn Stars*, in which history could be recalled by the bidding for Trail memorabilia, I might just have raised a flicker of interest.

But as a history of the makings of modern guerrilla warfare which besets us all today, I found no takers! And without our history, what are we?

Acknowledgements

ON THE COMPLETION OF a book or a film documentary or any endeavour where the lonely writer looks for encouragement, there comes the realization of how much is owed to so many others. Indeed, this book would not have been at all possible, or viable, without the ever-ready assistance of University of Toronto librarian staff, and especially that of Brock Silversides, Head of Media Commons, who has so diligently preserved my personal collection of films, photos, and documents essential to the telling of times long past.

It must be stressed that no one at CBC, either currently or in the past, has participated in any way in this narrative, nor had knowledge of its content. Even so, among the many friends of CBC (of whom I am one!) are friends of mine who in recent decades have forged a network second to none.

In the equally vital and talented realm of independent television production, my thanks and applause to hundreds of colleagues — producers, directors, editors, researchers, and camera crews — who made possible so many shared achievements, and in particular, not least for their constant kindness, my gratitude to film researcher Elizabeth Klinck and Hall-of-Fame executive producer Bob Culbert. With equal respect and appreciation, I salute the exceptional programmers who kick-started Canada's foremost documentary channels, History and Discovery, at the former Cindy Witten, Sydney Suissa, John Gill, and Michael MacMillan, and at the latter Trina McQueen and Paul Lewis. And from earlier years at CTV, my thanks for the treasured friendship and news savvy of Tom Gould and Don McQueen, and likewise a grateful recognition of Ian

McLeod and Mike Feheley as key to the success of *Vietnam: The Ten Thousand Day War*.

Never forgotten are friends and helpers during my many Vietnam visits, in some instances their names changed to protect sources. Ever in memory, I think of Visnews Tokyo representative Bob Nakai, the key "fixer" in getting me into North Vietnam, the start of a friendship that would long outlast the war, and also ever in memory the heroic Japanese global minded Yasuo Yanagisawa.

For their professionalism and for being such stalwarts, a special salute to Ivan Dolynskyj; to my travel companions in recent years, director of photography Mike Ellis and sound technician John Martin; and for getting me through those years my (hopefully lasting) thanks to some very dedicated surgeons and physicians: Dr. Marvin Waxman, Dr. Barry B. Rubin, Dr. Sidney B. Radomski, Dr. Barry P. Sniderman, and Dr. Frank Kalamut. And for supporting this book, my appreciation to Dundurn publishers and their staff, especially for the patience and ideas of editor Allister Thompson, editor Britanie Wilson, and publicist Jim Hatch.

And yet, despite all of the above, this book has been possible foremost because of the love and closeness of family — of my caring wife Mariko, my ever-compassionate daughter (award-winning author) Kyo, and son-in-law musician Dave Wall, as well as for the love and wondrous smiles of grandsons Yoshi and Mika, and for the love and encouragement of my brothers Andrew and Robin Maclear. Any book based on a personal lifetime is essentially an expression of debt owed to a great many others.

INDEX

Numbers that appear in italics refer to images and their captions.

PRAISE FOR MICHAEL MACLEAR'S
VIETNAM: THE 10,000 DAY WAR (1981)

Recently named (2008) by a *Guardian* critic
as the best non-fiction book about the war

"… It is hard to imagine how Maclear's effort could be bettered."
—*Montreal Gazette*

"… A clear, concise history, told with skill and understanding."
—*Toronto Star*

"… concise, dramatic, well organized…"
—*Los Angeles Times*

"… oral history at its best…"
—*Globe & Mail*

"The strength of the book is the way it tells how the tragedy evolved."
—*(London) Times* educational supplement

"… a blistering account of the Vietnam adventure."
—*Publishers Weekly*

"It's a gripping tale —
depressing, tragic, bewildering even after all this time."
—*Newsweek*

OF RELATED INTEREST

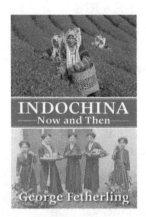

Indochina Now and Then
by George Fetherling
978-1554884254
$24.99

In *Indochina Now and Then*, George Fetherling recounts multiple journeys through Vietnam, Laos, and Cambodia, keeping an eye peeled and an ear cocked for whatever faint traces of French rule might remain. While doing so he searches diligently in village markets, curio shops, and rubbish bins, not to mention bookstalls along the Seine in Paris, for early picture postcards of Southeast Asia, the sort that native Frenchmen and Frenchwomen sent home to Europe.

The book is illustrated with sixty such images, most of them taken before the First World War. They evoke vanished ways of life in these exotic "lands of charm and cruelty" that have survived the wars and turmoil of the late twentieth century to emerge, smiling enigmatically, as the friendly face of free-market socialism. In its prose and pictures, *Indochina Now and Then* is a travel narrative that will leave an indelible impression in the reader's imagination.

Available at your favourite bookseller

Visit us at
Dundurn.com
@dundurnpress
Facebook.com/dundurnpress
Pinterest.com/dundurnpress

Printed in the USA
CPSIA information can be obtained
at www.ICGtesting.com
JSHW082203140824
68134JS00014B/406